A RABBI IN MAINE

A Rabbi in Maine

Harry Z. Sky

Quiet Waters Publications
Bolivar, Missouri
2009

For information contact:
    Quiet Waters Publications
    P.O. Box 34, Bolivar MO 65613-0034.
    E-mail: QWP@usa.net.
For prices and order information visit:
    http://www.quietwaterspub.com

Cover photo: Tom Jones

ISBN 1-931475-38-5
ISBN 978-1-931475-38-9
Library of Congress Control Number: 2008939932

CONTENTS

"Wherever I lived, I experienced adventurous living. I'm convinced it was due to what my mother called the maziq in me. I constantly sensed potential. I never felt that the moment I was living in was the final, telling moment of my life."

GROWING UP

In considering my current life situation, I feel the time has come to share my innermost self with friends and family. From my earliest memories, "family and friends" was an all-embracing title. At times in my earliest childhood, "family and friends" consisted of the visible and invisible. I knew quite early that there was more than the eye sees, and more than I sense and behold.

One day when I was quite young, I was sitting in my father's little hovel. It was a one-room structure, its shelves lined with books and various paraphernalia, used and indulged in by practicing Jews. My mother was there. My father had left the room, and I was seated in the right hand corner, an inflated balloon in one hand, and a Hebrew book was lying on the floor on my left side. I recall it as if it were today, my ripping pages from the book. Not tearing them, but ripping them. The pages were not torn. They were complete. They could be gathered and made into another book. My mother looked on in amazement and said, *Er ist a roter maziq*. He is a red spirit. A *maziq* is a spirit who stirs up the otherwise quiet, placid moment. A *maziq* is a force or person that appears without being announced. A *maziq* is a catalyst. A *maziq* is an instigator. A *maziq*'s very presence turns the quiet water into raging seas. I have wondered about that moment in my young life. What did my mother see? What did she experience, prompting her to call or label me a *maziq*?

Many years later, I had a dream. I dreamt I was a pixie, a celestial figure, who like a bee, tastes this honeycomb and then another, deriving nourishment and pollen to seed another field or plant. On the side stood a tall impressive figure. I sensed I was in the presence of a God figure. Perhaps Zeus, or another of the mystical figures. The nymph circled Zeus, and then suckled it and flew away. It suckled Zeus three more times and departed. When I dreamt that dream, I was in the midst of my own inner analysis. It wasn't a waking image that sometimes appears in your head, in your conscious moments, but an image – a dream story, stemming from my most inner depths. Within a few days of the dream, I recalled the *maziq*-spirit incident referred to above. I heard myself say, "is this what momma had in mind?" I'd derive my inner food from celestial sources that I was not fed by ordinary diets. Yes, I said to myself. My reverie continued. I wasn't interested in destroying the past (the papers of the Hebrew book), but putting them aside intact, and adding to my spiritual (book) intake the godly food that abounds in this universe.

My father's American sojourn seldom reached his dream dimensions. He dreamt of being a scholar, lecturing in a Yeshiva (a place where Talmudic studies are pursued), a rabbi, attached to a congregation, or one consulted on matters of Jewish law and principle. His Talmudic erudition was acknowledged early in his life. At the age of 14 or 15, he had been orally examined by the Rakatshover Illui, Ha-Rav Rosen, then in Dvinsk. He was awarded a "Zettel" (a certificate) attesting to his having reached a high level of understanding in Talmudic learning. He cited this incident throughout his life as a major turning point. He spoke of it with a sense of great pride and accomplishment. When he arrived in America, he resided for six months at the home of his sister Feige and his brother in law Yaaqov Ben Zion ha-Kohein Mendelson. Rabbi Mendelson occupied a high place of respect in Newark's Orthodox Jewish community. My uncle realized my father's unpreparedness for life (he felt rightly so). My father's frame of reference was the "world of the Talmud", not the daily world of most of us. He resided not in the world of ego and persona, but rather in the land of mystery (*sod*) and hidden memories (*remez*). My uncle urged my father to study and master the field of *Shechitah*, the ritual slaughter of fowl and cattle. Thus, he said, he will make a living, perform sacred tasks (help provide kosher food) and achieve some status in life. This life never brought satisfaction to my father. All *shochtim*, ritual slaughterers, received their legitimacy from rabbinic supervision. As in the past, so in the present. Sides were formed, some *shochtim* expressed loyalty to my uncle, Rabbi Mendelson and some to his detractor, Rabbi Joseph Konowitz. The chicken dealers, who ostensibly employed the *shochtim*, also joined the political game. Some went with Mendelson and others with Konowitz. When a chicken market owner took sides, the *shochet* he employed was expected to follow suit. One day, my father's employer changed sides, expelled my father, and brought Mordecai Ehrenkranz as his *shochet*. My father felt a religious principle had been violated: *Hasagat gevul*—avoiding another's property. He picketed the market. He stood on a platform and berated the customers entering the premises. I was not quite two years old. I recall sitting in my carriage mimicking my father's exhortations. I said it in Yiddish, the language spoken at home. People passed him and one woman said the child is a budding rabbi or exhorter.

My father, forever loyal to my rabbi uncle, stood by his side, defending my uncle's decisions and differing deeply with my uncle's antagonist Rabbi Konowitz. My uncle numbered among his followers, old, established families in the orthodox Jewish community. Most of these families were of long-term European origin. In my uncle, they realized the epitome and symbol of Chasidism's influence upon this segment of Jewish life. Above all, he possessed the warmth and concern of the rabbi – the teacher, the master whose advice and wisdom is forever being sought. My father looked to his brother in law for guidance, care and compassion, and found it there.

My brother Chayim of blessed memory was born two years after me, almost to the day. At the age of two, he developed a cold, which in turn became pleurisy and double pneumonia. At first, it was diagnosed as bronchitis, when his condition continued down hill, my mother, of blessed memory, called on the expertise of her nieces, the daughters of Feige, Tante Rebbetzin and Feter Mendelson, the illustrious Rabbi Mendelson. Their daughter Elizabeth took one look at my brother and intervened. He has to be seen by Prof. "Doctor" Pasternak, the medical guru of that day. Through her many social connections, she reached him within a few hours. He came to our house, examined the child, and said he is in dire circumstances. He has pleurisy and double pneumonia. My father and my mother became hysterical. My father called my uncle and he took over. He said first and foremost, as believing Jews, we have to say, the physician Dr. Pasternak is a godsend. He has been specially appointed to see to the well being of the child. Whatever he suggested, you abide by it. My father held my uncle in great respect and calmed down immediately. Remember, I was four years old at the time, but my antennae were fully functioning. I listened to all conversations, I absorbed whatever I sensed. Dr. Pasternak told my parents, the child is too sick to be moved. We will transfuse him and prepare him for surgery. Can it be done in the house? Our house was quite modest. The largest piece of furniture was our dining room table. Pasternak called his office. His surgical nurse rushed down to our house and my mother donated her blood, hoping to save her child. The transfusion was performed on the dining room table. Pasternak told his nurse to prepare for surgery. Where will it be done? Here on this table. I remember the look of consternation on the nurse's face. An oxygen tank was brought into the dining room and whatever could be done to sterilize the room was done in great haste. My cousin Elizabeth moved in and remained with us for sixty days. My uncle the rabbi said, we must give the child another name. Among many Jews, *Shinui Hashem* (name changing) was central. In changing a name, one changes one's *mazal*. If you change your abode, then you affect the heavenly constellation – mozal – that is your guardian in life. *Shinu Hashem*, name change, leads to change of destiny. This idea most likely originated in ancient Babylonia, the country of Jewish exile or from the *chasidei Ashkenaz*, the German Jewish Pietists. Chayim was given an additional name, Alter—"older," aged, or senior—thus hoping to deter whatever evil forces are floating around. My uncle said the doctor is one form of healing, whatever we do brings another. For me it was an early example of spirit and science being partners in the human scheme. Dr. Pasternak removed three ribs from my brother's back to allow the draining of the pleura. His left lung had collapsed and one of his eardrums had been affected. Elizabeth sat at his bedside. Dr. Pasternak took my father aside and said to him, that we must restore the child's strength.

"I want you to feed him a daily dosage of lard."

My father was taken aback. "Lard? Pig's fat? In *my* house? Never!"

Elizabeth overheard the conversation. She immediately communicated with my uncle. He dropped whatever he was doing and rushed to the house and took my father aside, and said, "Have you forgotten, *piquach nefesh docheh et ha-kol* – the saving of life takes precedence over everything else? If necessary, you have to feed the child lard. Go buy a special pot, spoon, and plate and feed him. Remember the Doctor is god's messenger."

Of course, he dropped all objections. The "*rav,*" the only rabbi he respected has spoken and the "lard" prescription was put into effect. It was touch and go for my brother. I was shipped (literally) to my Tante Dvoshe in the Bronx, a borough of New York City.

Tante married late in life. Her husband, Asher, was a widower, left with an only child, a son, Laybel. To Tante, Laybel was the apple of her eye. I guess I became her "peaches and cream." Tante was my mother's half-sister. They shared the same mother, but had different fathers. I was moved to my mother's father, Tzvi Hirsh. He was a fiery redhead, as was I (mother said I was a red "spirit"). He acted as if he were driven by an unidentified force. In his frustration, he would shout, howl, and at times, according to Tante Dvoshe, was quite abusive. She sensed in me quite early, such a resident force and tried in her own inimitable way, to guide it into positive, constructive channels. To some extent, she succeeded. I learned in my long life that such a "force" can never be totally quieted. It seems to possess a life of its own. Try as I or anyone else may, it's as if this is my "karma" and my task in life is to "tame it" so that its energy ceases to be a "destroyer" but can be brought some way into the arena of the builder. This force tries to feed on itself, but every so often, it seeks energizing and replenishment elsewhere. At times, it seems the "force" finds its own voice, and it is our approach to life. At times, it leads one into "temptation." It sees and senses the flows of accepted and respectable living. Its criticism is sharp, poignant, and to the point. Unlike other critics or critiques, it shuns the company of the many and stands to one side, offering its insights to the world surrounding it.

Tante recognized my weaknesses and my strengths. She refused to judge or condemn. She stood by quietly at my side, forever encouraging me and complementing me for all I did and said. To her, my force needed to be harnessed. Once, in her frustration over my behavior and outbursts, she tried to confine me, even threatened punishment, but then broke down and said, "You are different; you are not like everyone else's child."

I lived with Tante for two years. In 1930, I returned home. I was five-and-a-half years old. My mother decided it was school time. I was enrolled in the 17th Street School. My teacher was Ms. Keesweather. The kindergarten schoolroom was a strange place. I couldn't communicate with them. Their language wasn't mine. In our home, we spoke Yiddish, not English. Being a "strange one," I clung to my mother's "apron strings." I didn't venture outside. I didn't participate in the neighborhood games. Ball games did not interest me, nor did the "kids" of the neighborhood. I was destined to be a loner, or as Tante said, different from all others. Ms. K, my kindergarten teacher, sensed my difference. She spoke to me in German, assuming the home-spoken Yiddish was a German dialect. All of these attempts of addressing my sense of difference were well meant, but none of them tapped into the spirit that was the purveyor of the sense of difference.

I say this in all sincerity. In fact, one night, I awoke from a dream. I shared a bed with my brother, Alter Chayim Yitzhak. I sat up in bed and cried out. My father ran into our bedroom, wondering what has occurred. I said "Don't you see? A dark shadow or presence was there." My father smiled, opened the window, and proved to me the object flopping in the wind was a piece of clothing my mother had put out to dry on the fire escape. I was placated for the moment. But inside of me, I knew there was a perpetual challenging force trying to pull me away from whoever or whatever I am at any given moment. Already, at the age of five or six, I knew this force had a mind of its own. It seemed to be part of me, and yet separate from me. It dictated or decided my daily agenda.

I completed the kindergarten phase of my early schooling and in the fall term of 1930, entered first grade. My teacher was Ms. Campbell. She was a big buxom woman, who approached her class of students as if they were her family. She chose me as king of the class, and Rose Kosofsky as queen. One day, she paraded the two of us on her shoulder as if to say here comes the king, and here comes the queen. Yet, she too, sensed the existence of the unbridled force and tried to tame it. One day, she concentrated her penmanship "hour" on perfecting our cursive signatures. Mine was considered poor. I couldn't write the capital "S" of "Sky" properly. After many attempts at correction, she gave up. She sat me in the coat closet until "I learned to write it properly." I knew it was not my fault. I tried to write the capital "S" correctly, but somehow my pen slipped, or I didn't write between the lines, or the "S" ended up looking like something else. It had a "dragon" quality to it. Needless to say, the discipline didn't succeed, and the form of the "S" remained imperfect for many years to come. Writing, like other moments, demanding dexterity, or better a sense of connectedness evaded me. My intuition said the force is in charge.

Problems of dexterity surfaced again and again. In those days of 1930 onward, physical education was central in public school education. It honed our sense of team, of group, of oneness with others. After school, neighborhood children would pair off, form teams, and try to excel in dexterous activities. I failed all physical education tests. My penmanship was disjointed, as were all attempts to throw a ball in a given direction, to climb a piece of gym equipment. Unlike other boys of my age, I felt isolated from all collective activity.

The force "ran the show." Its agenda seemed to be the world I sought. The world of my dreams was unlike the world of my contemporaries. Their world was an accommodation, conversely mine was in its latency saying *lo zu ha-derekh* – this isn't the road to be followed. If truth be told, there is more than meets the eye. Every moment, every act, every sentence recorded on paper or elsewhere, was poignant with meaning. Something other than the immediate experience is calling us. The force was attuned to this theme, and it tried to direct me towards it.

My years in public school were, to say the least, challenging. Upon completing the first grade, I was promoted to grade two. My teacher was Ms. Dougherty. She was a strict disciplinarian. She walked up and down the aisle with a thick ruler in her hand. We students were expected to sit at our desks, fingers linked to each other, head high, backs erect. If you were out of "line," she would tap you with her stick. Rose Kasofsky was promoted, and we spent the term together. I resisted and resented my teacher. One day, she tapped me with her ruler. I cried and ran to the Assistant Principal complaining the teacher "hit me." She sent me home. I complained to my mother and she brought me to the Assistant Principal's office. My mother in her broken English said she resented her child being physically disciplined. No one has the right to raise a hand to her child. Ms. Dougherty never touched me again. She had her moment of revenge. Rose Kasofsky skipped the third grade and entered the fourth grade. I missed the list. My state of being "special" suffered the defeat of rejection.

Somehow, I managed to survive the "slings and arrows of misguided fortune." My father ever mindful of his soul's future –decided early what my destiny should be. Since his universe was within the four cubits of *halakhah*" (Jewish tradition and folklore) he undertook to shape me, and steer me in that direction. At the early age of three, I was taught Hebrew. I was a proficient reader of the prayer book at 3 ½. In fact, when my brother Chayim was in the early stage of his illness, I remember taking a Siddur – a prayer book, doffing a *tallit* (a prayer shawl) and chanting Hebrew words, hoping they would help. I was drawing on the mysterious power in me for good and not for the activities generated by the force's seductive power.

My father, quite early in my life, sensed the power within me. My mother had dubbed me a red-haired *mazik* – uncontrolled force. My father saw it in another way. He said my brother Chayim, who later received a Masters Degree in mathematics was a "plugger" while I was the intuitive one. In fact, at the age of five, he taught me a *midrash*. I memorized it and spoke of its implications. I received a prize for the presentation. My family predicted I would be a *maggid*, an interpreter of text and life some day. As I look back at my life from the vantage of 84 years, the stories within me are clarified. Thus, I interpret the rabbinic tradition all of us possess many inclinations. The *Tov*, the good, or better, the natural *tov*, the natural good (Campbell-Bliss) inclination and the *Ra* or the-evils, or as I see it, the seductive, the voice that says it's okay, no matter what it may be. This latter voice seems to have the notion that some acts are okay for you (even when society, realism, or ego differs). Other things which society stresses, the persona aspect may be detrimental. During my earliest years, I felt the seductive voice had attained an upper hand in my life. It became my *reah*, my intimate friend. In weak moments, in insecure moments, the seductive voice stepped in, bent on alleviating my pain and relieving my loneliness.

The fourth grade brings me few remembrances. My peers became the heroes of the gym and the ball field, enthusiasts when playing king of the mountain. A selfish streak appeared and grew. We were all dubbed with nicknames and titles. My father assured me the same was done in his hometown in Latvia. Everyone had a nickname. Sometimes it encouraged its recipient; other times it denigrated the bearer. For a while, I was known as Red, Momma's boy for I always ran to my mother for protection and security.

During the fourth and fifth grade years, it became clearer and clearer. I was an outsider. I always wondered: How can I bridge me and the rest of the world? One day, I had an accident in my pants and ran home to momma for solace. Much happened during this period. Almost daily, incidents occurred and failing to be the controller, the victorious one, I was constantly cast in a negative role. It affected my entire outlook on life. I became short tempered, at times overcome by deep inner feelings. I felt surrounded by malevolent forces. The slightest sound frightened me. The simplest tasks overwhelmed me. At times, I wondered why this was happening. Am I on God's "to be punished" list? If so, of what am I guilty? Whom did I injure? One day, during the fourth grade year, I walked home with a "Chinese" student. Not knowing what to say to him, or how to address him, I said, without really thinking, "You are a chinky Chinaman." He was taken aback. His face was drawn. It could have been anger or hurt – I'm not sure which one it was. I knew I had hit a sensitive spot. He was tall, and I was short. I'd hoped he would be my friend, but my remark stood in the way. On another day, I spoke to another person of foreign descent. Maybe, he'd be my friend, but to no avail. I was rejected by both girls and boys.

I complained to my parents. My mother said it will work itself out (*es werd sich oyspresen*). My father said *shinui maqom shinui mazal* (a change of place will change your luck)—you need to go elsewhere. The debate between them continued for many months. In the meantime, my father attempted to introduce me into the realm of traditional knowledge or practice. We studied Chumash (the Pentateuch) and Rashi (the medieval commentator), Mishnah, the synoptic books of the Talmud. My father quoted over and over again the saying *Chash be-rosho yaasoq ba-torah*, "If something bothers you, drop what you are doing, and indulge in Torah study". This "safe cocoon" did not work. The loneliness persisted. I was more and more of an "oddball," and my problems multiplied.

One day on my way to school, I crossed the street and passed by two "patrol boys." They assisted at busy crossings and sometimes kept the traffic at bay. These particular patrol boys signaled and we crossed the street. As I passed one of them, he brushed against me. I looked up. He was staring straight ahead. I continued my trek to school. I went to class. One half hour later, the principal's office called and I was sent to the office. When I entered the office, I was told to come forward. I did.

The principal said, "empty your pockets." I did. I extracted a box of matches from one pocket. The principal looked at me. I was frightened, disheveled. Without questioning me, she said, "You're expelled from school. Leave the building immediately."

I cried. "Why? What have I done?"

She told me not to persist in lying. "You intended to set fire to this place."

I was utterly confused. "No, no," I cried.

"Where did you get these matches?"

"I don't know; they are not mine."

"You are a liar, a cheat, a troublemaker. Out!" I ran home crying all the way.

My mother greeted me at the door, *"Wos is geshehn?"*— What happened?

Between sobs, I told her I had been expelled from school.

"Why, what did you do?"

"Nothing. Nothing!"

Her facial expression informed me of her response. *Here we go again.* When will this end? One bit of trouble after another. *Why can't you be like the other boys in the neighborhood?*

Mama doffed her hat and coat and we trudged off to the principal's office. She wouldn't speak to us and the vice principal intervened. Between tears, she sensed my pain and frustration. She turned to my mother and said, "Mrs. Sky, I fear your son doesn't fit into our school community. Perhaps you should consider another form of education for him."

"But why? I am an American citizen and so are my children. Why must they go to another school?"

The Vice Principal shrugged her shoulders. That night when Poppa came home from the chicken market, my parents conversed anxiously in Russian (for whenever they sought privacy, that was their language of communication). Remember this occurred in the latter part of the fifth grade. The school had made up its mind. The recommendations of the authorities were etched in stone.

My father (and in some ways, my mother, too) were quite aware of bureaucratic tendencies. But they also recognized their inconsistencies. From earliest days, prior to election days (November and June), a ward captain would knock on our door. One day, it was a Democratic representative, on another, a Republican. They would greet my mother and say, "*Chayke* (Ida), it's time to vote. You know for whom to vote." And she would say, "Yes." The Democrat man and the Republican representative would leave five dollars on the table. My mother's response was, "What a great country! They even sometimes leave enough money to buy the groceries."

My mother had the eye of an artist and the heart of a constant caregiver. The Depression hit us in 1929. I was five years old at the time, and it inaugurated a difficult economic period for our family and most others we knew. My mother's half-brother, Feter Chloyne (or "Uncle Charles") had a very successful store of Hebrew books and religious objects in the Bronx. He was a leader in community undertakings. When the Depression arrived, he lost everything. Tante Dvoshe who lived near by claimed he was in the stock market. My mother denied it. He moved out of the Bronx and spent some time in Cleveland, and then moved into our apartment. My brother Chayim and I loved him. He challenged our imagination. On festival days, he'd produce scenes representative of the festival's history. For instance, one year he made a Shavuot tableau. It was, according to Jewish tradition, the anniversary of the giving of the Ten Commandments. Feter Chloyne, Uncle Charles, took some raw eggs, pinpricked them, and drew out the liquid. He took some dough and shaped wings, making them into birds. They were strung up on the chandelier and as the wind blew, they circled around and around. Feter Chloyne told us they were the birds that circled the mountain when our ancestors received the Ten Commandments. On Chanukah, he created a tableau of the Maccabees battling the Syrian Greeks. Every day was another experience and our young ripe imaginations responded to his prodding.

The realm of the imagination was my earthly Garden of Eden. I felt, I heard, I sensed unseen forces. Every day, I knew my personal "angel" was at my side. (Many, many years later a psychic told me I was under a "protective cloud.") I recall an incident. I was eight or nine years old and my father and I were studying Chumash (Pentateuch). Our text, "Jacob left Be'er-Sheva on the way to Charan." He arrived at a given place, and slept there. He dreamt of *malakhim* (angels) ascending and descending a ladder that reached into the upper spheres. Rashi comments that the messenger who accompanied Jacob was returning to the upper spheres and others were descending to get ready for the next part of the journey. My father and I discussed this commentary. I asked him, "Do I have any *malakhim* at my side. Do angels protect us too?"

He said, "Of course."

"What do they look like?" (I was a precocious child).

"They may look like you and me." I was puzzled. He explained: "*Ha-Qadosh Barukh Hu* (The Holy One, Blessed is

He) has many angels. They are dressed in different garbs. Sometimes you recognize them and at other times you don't."

I did not pursue this thought.

My imagination was quite old, but my ability to express my inner thoughts was limited. Even at that early age, I sensed my isolation and it affected all I did in the day-to-day world. But within, I knew and sensed and believed in a world of protecting spirits. Recently, I drove through the Rhine Valley in Germany up to the Black Forest. In the forest, I sensed "spirits" ready to converse with me.

Throughout my childhood, my father referred to the spirits, the *shaydim* one can find them listed in various places in the Talmud and the neo-Kabbalist literature. He deeply believed in their presence. My mother was attuned to the feminist aspect of the spirit world. Both of them, father and mother, sensed their relationship to the spirits and we the children were raised with *shaydim*, "spirit" lessons. We were three brothers. I believe I was the most mystically inclined.

In the sixth grade, I was promoted to a teacher, Ms. O'Connor, with fiery red hair. She tried to teach us fractions and other mixed mathematical situations. She insisted in categorization. Whole numbers, under whole numbers, fractions under fractions, oranges under oranges, etc.

The "semi-world" was foreign to her and the "whole" world was foreign to me. I felt the distance between the two worlds, and even more so, the world around me and the world within me. My father sensed my strength. Together with my mother, they decided I should leave Newark and go study at a *yeshivah* (a school for Talmudic studies). My father's rationale was simple: In the world of the Talmud one finds answers to soul questions, unlike the secular schools. My mother felt in the *yeshivah* I would find people with interests similar to mine. I acquiesced and on one fine fall day in 1936, I went to New York City and remained there.

In hindsight, my parents were correct. Young persons who in their parents' eyes were unfit for the secular world were there. But the answers they sought, the language they yearned for, the symbols prepared to strengthen their spirit was sometimes taken captive by the negative nature more than the positive side of life. Among the students were budding scholars, but that same body had its collection of the lost, the dreamers, individuals who missed the "boat," and the adjusted ones. I felt I was of the former class. My boat had left shore and I was stranded.

After completing the sixth grade— with its harrowing experience of the matches—my father said to my mother, "he must be brought into a completely Jewish environment, the *yeshivah* (school for Talmudic studies)." When approached, I agreed even though I feared it. After all, it was an escape. This was the beginning of an approach to life. When faced with a challenge, don't force it, or seek an escape route. The trip to the yeshiva had a strange quality about it. I recall the trip. We boarded in New York City, an open-side trolley. I remember hanging on to a step to keep from falling and losing balance. I felt as if I was entering a mysterious world, surrounded by my stories, beings, forces, and sounds. The clang of the trolley bell had an aura of its own. It wasn't just the clang, but something else surrounded and clung to it. I felt I was caught in that undefined atmosphere. We arrived at the *yeshivah*, and I was given a short test to see how well versed I was in Talmud study. I don't think I passed with flying colors. I was placed in Pansky's class – an elementary Talmud class.

I was assigned a seat behind a scruffy boy. After 10-20 minutes, he turned his head sideways and whispered out of the side of his mouth, "Do you want to buy some stamps?"

I didn't know what to answer. I'd never collected postage stamps and didn't know the difference or worth of one or another. Yet, I was hungry for friendship. I felt I'd been dragged into this place.

At home, no one bothered to talk to me, to help me sort out my feelings, hopes, or beliefs. For even at that early age, I realized home was an area of the beyond or, as we say, the supernatural. God was constantly mentioned. Poppa *davened* (traditional prayer) daily. He doffed his *talit* (prayer shawl) and *tefilin* each morning. He never neglected *minchah* (the afternoon prayer) or *maariv* (the evening prayer). For him, a day didn't go by without a regimen of daily study. He was a pious Jew in the classic sense, and wanted that for me. I resisted. I couldn't automatically drift into this kind of faith. I asked myself (and everyone) else: Why? I couldn't forbid myself in any avenue of action or discourse. This attitude has lasted for me all my life. I've been the eternal seeker and experimenter. In fact, I began to feel, in this pre-puberty stage, messages were coming my way, no matter what it may be – the young guy trying to sell me stamps or anything else that may arise. If truth be told, this is my uniqueness and the source of my, at times, questionable behavior. What I missed most of all was a foundation arrived at in concert with my parents, that was my own. On that fateful day on the open trolley, I think I sensed I wasn't going into my own world, but a world of my father's creation and imagination. In classic Jewish thought, the way of the uncertain always received special recognition. Honor your father and mother, meant just that: Accept, acknowledge their way beyond question, with great respect.

In the Talmud, a story is told of a convert to Judaism and his act of respect. One of the gems that adorned the temple high priest's breast plate was damaged and had to be replaced. After much inquiry, the Temple authorities discovered an exact duplicate in a non-Jew's possession. The Temple authorities debated, "How can we approach him? He was a parent of another convert of the community. Would he part with the gem? Would he hesitate to sell it and thus aid and abet the struggle of conflicting communities, conflicting points of view? Someone said, but his son is a convert, let's approach him. The son hesitated. His father was an elderly man, slept most of the day; this gem was always in sight, either on his bedside table or underneath his pillow. The son, cited the fifth commandment, honoring one's parents, and said, "I cannot disturb him." One of the scholars of the temple community said, the son was right. We'll have to await the father consenting moment, not our own, for the honoring of parents is the assurance of better communities.

I knew all of this. I'd heard these stories innumerable times. Often, it was my parents' (especially my father's) escape route. All differences were answered the same way. That's one way, I, your father, won't let it be—a perfect combination for an insecure childhood. After many years of studying and pondering, I feel the ultimate error of western child raising stems from this attitude of mind: "Children should be seen and not heard."

My father tried to further his stance by describing his relationship to my grandfather. He was a learned man. In days gone by, he would have been known as the town scholar. In fact, my father told me he was the twenty-ninth generation of such scholars, and he hoped I'd be the thirtieth. His father had not been employed by any synagogue or community organization. His adage was, "Don't let your learning become a tool by which to amass any material gain." His feeling was learning for its own sake.

My father told me whenever his father returned from the mill—from which he derived a living, he (my father) would don his shoes to greet him with greatest respect. As if to say, "why wasn't I that way?" In retrospect, I can say having "failed to find my way" in the world at pre-puberty, I gave in and said to myself, "Let's try it his way."

From the first day, the *yeshivah* was a rude awakening. All of us, preadolescents seemed to feel the pain and isolation. Our adolescent needs were ignored. Discussion of our sexuality was taboo. In fact, all hints of budding sexual expression were suppressed. Whenever physical needs or drives arose, we were advised to immerse ourselves in text, in learning, in the intellectual skills of Talmudic study. When, in the study of Talmud, we encountered texts alluding to human or animal reproduction, they were skipped over. *Bi'ah*, the Hebrew term for sexual intercourse, was avoided, skipped, or ignored whenever it was encountered, even though it was plainly there in the text. Some of the students, streetwise in their knowledge of intimate behavior, found sexual partners among themselves. Others gravitated to heterosexual situations. Any way chosen was considered *nibul*—disgusting, degrading, something to be avoided or repressed. Abstinence was urged, but intimacy was practiced.

Attempts were made in the *yeshiva* for older students to teach the principles of the *musar* (moralistic) movement, a form of repression, the idea being that ordinary human needs and desires, in fact, all physical in nature, were degrading. The person who practiced repression, keep the needs, the yearnings, the drives under wraps, was the hero. The one who paid attention to his yearnings and drives was a *menuval*, a degenerate. It was black and white, with no room for gray.

Few *yeshivah* authorities understood or appreciated the inherent desire for physical contact (*negiah*, touching) in adolescent years. Few were cognizant of the yearnings of the heart. Among *Chasidim* (spiritually conscious Jews), such as the followers of Rabbi Nachman of Bratslav, attention was paid to the behaviors of the older teenagers. We have extant writings of Rabbi Nachman and the exercises he prescribed for the young ones: what to do when caught up in sexual drives or desires.

In my case the loneliness and the fear felt by me triggered the receptivity to sexual answers. The fear and the loneliness made me a possible subject for such solutions. The sexual tension was always in the air. The community consisted of two groups. Those who resolved their tensions, their insecurities in classic ways: The first was *chash be-rosho, yaasoq be-torah*—one who suffers from malaise (fear and loneliness) let him indulge or become involved in matters of Torah (sacred knowledge). Solve the problem by studying. The second group consisted of those who fell prey to their tensions, their anxieties, and sought raw answers (power, sex, etc.). I sensed the inner turmoil within myself, gravitating from one "pole" to another—raw power, tension, feeling on one hand, and immersion in text on the other. Text didn't consist of words, printed material alone. Text implied stories of pious victories, of individuals with super power, the strength, and the ability to overcome the tension. The power was derived not from military and destructive powers, but more often from the "word." God's power says the Midrash isn't derived from physicality but from the power of the word: "God spoke and the world came into being."

For many years, life in our household centered on the world of my brother, Chayim. Being of strong character, of mettle, he sought a way out of the "sick one" syndrome. The wider world was his answer. I, on the other hand, felt deprived, and found myself taking on the persona of the *oy vey* (constant sadness), the needy one. I developed an "actor's shell." I feigned neediness, since at least it brought Momma's concern and attention. My confusion grew with leaps and bounds. Our true family celebrations seemed to be of two strains: Momma's in the Bronx at Tante Dvoshe's home and Feter Chloyne, and Poppa's, at the Mendelsons'. In a self-conscious way, I felt closer to the Bronx celebrations. Since my birthday was Erev Pesach—the night before Passover, I had the special task of distributing the sweets at one end of the *Seder* (the Passover meal and celebration). It took place in Feter Chloyne's house.

Poppa regarded "Bobleh" momma's mother, as the epitome of piety. She sat on her chair at the head of the stairs, a *shayfel* on her head and a *tehilim* or *tzaynah v'raynah* in her hands. She mumbled the words. She was frail, hunch backed. Momma later developed the same back posture. Chloyne and Dvoshe were half-brother and half-sister to momma. She had two full brothers, who lived in the Bronx. Once I met one of them. There was obviously distance between the full brothers and Momma.

I remember the day Bobleh died. It was a Shabbat afternoon. Poppa and I had gone to the Sephardic *beit midrash* (synagogue) for *minchah* (afternoon prayer). We were summoned home. Poppa made *tordalah* at Bobleh's bedside and she expired. She was taken off the bed and placed on the floor with four candles (two at her head, and two at her feet).

The *taborah* (purification rite for the dead) in preparation for the next day's burial took place in the house. Chayim and I were turned over to some family member and didn't attend the funeral. Momma suffered a breakdown immediately after the funeral. I remained behind with Dvoshe. The details are murky. As I mentioned earlier, when Chayim had his bout with pleurisy and double pneumonia, I was sent to live with Dvoshe. Dvoshe became the haven for me. Home away from home. It didn't matter. Wherever I resided, I felt there was another home available to me. It was populated by images, inanimate creatures turned animate. It took on human form like the stories I heard and were read to me, they became real and alive.

Once (I must have been two or three years old at this point) before Chayim's illness, I had an accident. Dvoshe took me into her bathroom and beat me with a rope. I never spotted myself again. In many ways, she was a *Kali* person, loving yet disciplining. She always took me into her bed. It had a down cuddly blanket. Her body was warm and friendly. In later years, I went into Momma's bed, cleaned the bed-posts of the bed bug eggs, and cleaned her ears of any wax lying there. It wasn't a "normal" upbringing – clinging to one or the other.

Feter Chloyne suffered during the Depression. He lost his communal stance, his bookstore, and his real estate. His wife, Tante Dvoshe, took a vow that all of their creditors will be paid "to the last penny," and she kept her word. The day her husband died, she paid the last bill. I was five years old when the Bobeh died, and fifteen when Feter Chloyne died. In both cases, the path of death intrigued and puzzled me. Where have they gone? Will I ever hear from them and see them again?

I entered public school at the age of five. My teacher was Ms. Keeswater. She was of German extraction. At that time, my English speaking skills were halting. Yiddish, Russian, and

Hebrew were our home languages. Since I was the oldest child, I became for my parents, the extension of the old country. The culture shared with me was old country vintage. The customs, the ceremonies, the diet, all of it "old country." Ms. Keeswater, during the first ninety days of the term, conversed with me in German. My Yiddish facility assisted me whenever she spoke with me. I vaguely remember those days. Kindergarten was playtime. We learned very little. Colors, shapes, numbers were interesting concepts, but I felt (as I had for some time), it wasn't the essence of things. Somehow, different ideas and knowledge were being conveyed at home. The whispering about Feter Mendelson's problems, the hinting about Feter Chloyne's downfall. I don't recall the exact date, but suddenly Tante Kleine Dvoshe moved out of our house. She didn't like me, nor did I like her. As soon as I began public school, I felt I was an outsider – no friends, no companions, no sharing in sports, nor in humor and ideas. I went from school to home, and immediately went to Momma's side. Once, Momma took out a deck of cards and taught me how to play Casino. We heard Poppa's footsteps on the stairs and the cards were quickly stored away. Poppa was opposed to such frivolity. I recall in her earlier years, Momma had a gay demeanor, and Poppa had a solemn one.

One day, when I was in the second grade, my teacher (reputedly a former prison guard) was passing up and down the aisle, stick in hand. It was good-posture time. We were expected to sit like automatons, our hands neatly folded. If Ms. Donahue disapproved of your posture or hand position, she'd rap your knuckles. She once rapped mine and blood was exuding from the broken skin. I cried and ran out of the classroom. I had to stay for detention.

Upon getting home, I told Momma about it. She took me by the hand and we went to the Vice Principal's office. The teacher was called and when confronted with the incident, she said to the Vice Principal, "Will you give credence to this green horn, or will you accept the testimony of a *bona fide* American?" The Vice Principal was disturbed. She tried to make peace, but my mother wouldn't be placated. She related the incident to Poppa and his response was, "When did a *goy* (non-Jew) ever care for a Jew?" It was the beginning of his campaign of preparing me for the "Jewish World" of the *ye-shivah* life. My isolation grew.

In the third and fourth grades, we were introduced to gym. It meant jumping, running, throwing balls. I'm convinced I lacked coordination. I couldn't throw, catch, or run. I failed anything and everything that called for athletic or coordinate skills. I recall vividly a moment in gym. We were lined up to perform three tasks: climbing ropes, maneuvering the horse, and running/jumping over objects. I sensed my inability to accomplish these tasks. I resigned myself to the idea. It wasn't my cup of tea, and lost all interest in sports and sport competition. The gym teacher paid attention to the skillful ones. The rest of us were discards in his eyes.

But nature abhors a vacuum. So, I sought other outlets, outer companions. My brother Dave says I gravitated to the *maydlach*, sought the company of women. He was born in March, 1933, so he would have been conscious of my presence by 1935-1936. I was 11 or 12 years old at that time.

The infamous incident of the matches took place, I think, in sixth grade in 1935. Almost immediately after that, Poppa proposed that I would go to MTJ. I accepted. Schoolwise, it was horrible – dingy rooms, dingy dorm, dingy food, and terrible, terrible loneliness. It must have been in spring 1937 when Y. W. approached me and I accepted his "invitation." I was caught up for many years in that energy, only now realizing all of its ramifications. If there is anything positive after all of this, it opened my eyes to the false god I had chosen. Instead of seeing libido or creative energy, it was king Phallos who took center stage – right out of Freud's text book. It took me many years of analysis to realize this is not my god and it is not what I was looking for. The years from 1937 until today have been my wilderness years. That memory and anything that reinforced it and never stopped to ask if this was truly what I need, is this truly what I seek. Y.W. approached me after my Bar Mitzvah. I couldn't care less about anything in those days except the "phallic energy," one promiscuous moment after another. Yet never allowing myself to fall into the permanent trap of the other. The trap? Nothing else is of interest to me - the way of the totally addicted. I bordered on it, but still had moments of withdrawal from all that.

I remember the day Poppa and I went to MTJ. We traveled on an open side trolley car. When we arrived there, I was put into Rabbi Pinsky's class. It was a strange atmosphere. It didn't remind me of any school I ever attended. I was assigned to a seat. I didn't have a clue about the Rabbi's teaching. It was boring, that much I knew, but what was it about? I had no clue or interest in the material being studied and taught. Within minutes, the boy in front of me turned around and offered me some used stamps. I bought them. Why? I was hoping to "establish" a friendship. I was immediately dubbed as a stupid yokel and sucker. I had no identity. No one knew me. I can't remember where I slept the first night – at the *yeshivah*, at Tante Dvoshe's – I'm not sure. In all, I spent three years at MTJ. Poppa came to visit me a few months or weeks later.

Pensky tested me and, of course, I didn't know anything. I received the first report card from the "secular" department. I failed and destroyed the card. When Poppa came that first time, the teacher wanted to know why he never signed the card and why it wasn't returned to him. Poppa said he never received it. Nothing was said to me, to him, no punishment. My Bar Mitzvah was imminent. Poppa prepared a *derash* (Talmudic homily) and I was expected to memorize and deliver it. Pensky reviewed it with me. The Bar Mitzvah took place on the second day of Pesach. I began my *derash* and, at some early point, inevitably said, "Oops, I made a mistake!" and started again. A few weeks later, on *Lag Bomer*, we had a party at home. Tante Dvorshe, Tante Chanach, and Momma cooked. The furniture was moved out of Momma and Poppa's bedroom (we lived on 17th Street in those days.) I got forty dollars in gifts and Poppa and Momma took it to pay for the food. Everyone spoke. There were forty guests. I received a set of Silverman *chumashim* (Pentateuch) from England. Cousin Nehemiah gave me a Waltham pocket watch, some clothes, and a pen.

I went back to MTJ after Pesach. In June, Diamond (a Newarker) stood there with the square *yarmulke* (skullcap) like his father's on his head. It was lovely, of course, and I was jealous, arousing great anxiety. Poppa said that, when he was my age, his Talmudic knowledge was sharp and honed – so why couldn't I be that way? He never had the luxury of a bed. He slept in the *beit midrash* (synagogue), because that was the only place available to him. I at least had a bed at MTJ, at a private home, at Dvoshe's. At first, I'd ride to Manhattan with Osher, Dvoshe's husband. But then he lost his job, and I had to go by myself.

"This kid is sitting there and he takes out his wallet and he takes out a bunch of photographs that he took. They had piles and piles and piles of corpses in the trains, the unburied mounds of people. I don't remember all the details, but this left such a horrible impression."

AFTER THE WAR

I entered the seminary in 1946 and was elected to my first pulpit in 1948. This period of time was right after World War II. I was involved in protest meetings, and I remember towards the end of the war there was a rumor making the rounds that the Germans were ready to trade Jews for trucks. For a truck you'd get "x" number of Jews. There were some people who picked that up and there was a real effort to raise a fantastic sum of money to buy as many trucks so we could possibly get and rescue as many Jews as possible.

Those years touched every one of us. It was wrenching, absolutely wrenching. We knew terrible things were happening but who knew the full dimensions of it? How could you?

My first experience with someone who managed to get away was in 1938. I was 14 years old. One Friday night, a man appeared in our synagogue. He had come from Vienna and he had lived in that section of Vienna which was the most heavily populated Jewish section, 15th-16th Bezirk. I remember that scene back in my mind's eye right now, walking home from *shul* with him, telling me how he had to give up everything to get out.

At the time I didn't understand what he was talking about. But later on I read what was done to strip the Viennese, the Austrian Jews, of their possessions. "You'd come in, first thing, you'd come to a table, you show them your pass. They took it away from you. Then you had to give them an inventory of everything you had. If you lied—and if they caught you lying—you were shot. Then you had to turn in whatever you had on you, valuables, jewelry, whatever. By the time you were at the end of the table, all you had was the shirt on your back and maybe ten shillings."

When they came to this country, the Jewish community was organized. No one was left hungry. They were taken care of. We found jobs for them. We educated their children.

In 1946 I had a fantastic experience. I had entered the seminary as an auditor in January of 1946. I had graduated Yeshiva (college) in 1945 and I took some time off, preparing for seminary. In June of 1946 I walked down Broadway from the seminary at 122nd Street to 100st Street to a kosher restaurant for dinner. I sat down at a table and there were two young people, sitting opposite me. Young, yet they looked old. There was something weird about it. And I don't know why, to this day, I can't tell you why, I automatically struck up a conversation with them in Yiddish. At the Yeshiva, I spoke in Yiddish only when we were studying, not conversationally. As it turns out, these two people were brother and sister. They had arrived in the United States just that day. At the end of the war, President Truman went beyond the quotas and allowed 1,000 displaced persons to come from Europe to the United States. They were two of the thousand. They were housed in two hotels in New York. One was the hotel *Marseilles*, three blocks away from that restaurant. That's why they were eating there.

This kid is sitting there and he takes out his wallet and he takes out a bunch of photographs that he took. They had piles and piles and piles of corpses in the trains, the unburied mounds of people. I don't remember all the details, but this left a horrible impression. I went back to the hotel with them. I had never seen such turmoil in my life.

There were some social workers working with them, but these people were so agitated running back and forth, back and forth, back and forth, not just these two people, but everybody else that was there. There were others, too. Finally, one of them gave me a list of names of people who were still looking for relatives in the United States. Well, I called these names in to a Yiddish newspaper. We brought some of the displaced persons over to the seminary. We took them to a Russian movie. Boy, if anything opened my eyes to what those horrible years were about, this did. They started telling me these stories.

One kid, 16 years old, looked like a dwarf. Why? During the whole time, he was hidden in the cellar. Never saw sunshine from 1939 to 1945, from the age of 10 to 16. Apparently, without Vitamin D from the sun, his bones failed to grow properly. He was lucky to survive. I met a woman and her daughter. They looked pretty, blonde and as Nordic as anybody could possibly be. The two of them had passed in Poland for non-Jews. That's how they survived. I mean stories, and stories, and stories, during this Holocaust. And now, I think there are memories. What can I say? These are very personal to me.

I feel like I contributed to things like that not happening again. I became involved with civil rights. There's no such thing as saying this one has a right to live and that one doesn't. I don't buy that.

"I challenged the traditionalists among them in many ways. First, I felt Judaism's message wasn't for Jews alone. From that sprang the beginnings of my ultimate belief that the New Testament is a kind of midrash al-ha-Tanakh, a gloss on the Old Testament."

EARLY MINISTRY

After seminary, I was called to Gloucester, Massachusetts, the first real attempt on my part to live in the real world. I had an active rabbinate. Two months after I arrived in Gloucester, the Sisterhood sponsored an evening of food and fun. Prior to the event, I wandered into the kitchen and noticed the mixing of meat and dairy utensils. I said to the chairperson that to keep a kosher kitchen, one must separate the two— meat from dairy, dairy from meat, utensils, pots and pans. For this audacity, I was "called onto the carpet."

The vice president said I was there on false pretenses. "We're not Orthodox," he said. "Why must we be bound by these archaic laws?"

Being young, a novice in the field, I was offended and walked out of the room, but eventually I was called back and a truce was arrived at. A month or two later, we invited this same vice president, whose name was Kerr, to our home for *Shabbat* dinner on a Friday night. We served a roast bought from Swachmann, a kosher butcher in Boston. Ben Kerr cut into the roast lying on his plate and said, "Rabbi, I thought you kept kosher. This is too good to be kosher!" I tried to explain to him our shopping habits—the kosher butcher, the Hebrew book store, our regular shopping forays into Filene's Basement—as if to say, "I'm as American as you are." Our eating habits may differ but our daily human routine is similar to yours. We, too, seek the best meat cuts. The image of the Rabbi in Gloucester was the *kol bo*, the general Jewish facto-tum. He was the *shochet* (ritual slaughterer), the *melamed* (He-brew schoolteacher), the *shaliach tzibur* (leader at services)— never a Rabbi, always a reverend. I, on the other hand, was the first "American" Rabbi to have served their congregation.

The synagogue building was formerly the Universalist Church of Gloucester. It had a pump organ behind the pul-pit. On the wall above the organ was graffiti—mostly the names of former organ pumpers. Among those was one named Roger Babson. He donated books to the synagogue and was always inquiring about its current situation.

I made many marks in that community. I challenged the traditionalists among them in many ways. First, I felt Judaism's message wasn't for Jews alone. From that sprang the beginnings of my ultimate belief that the New Testament is a kind of *midrash al-ha-Tanakh*, an attempt to extract hidden meanings in the Old Testament. People sensed it. They said, "Why can't you be as clear in the synagogue as you are in the churches? Why are you a religious humanist *away* from the synagogue, and a troubled, anxious one *in* the synagogue, forever battling the Jewish authorities and forever acting as if you were a prisoner trying to break free from his shackles. In a light moment, I jestingly explained that no one in the churches targeted me.

In the 1950s and 60s, Jews were seeking ways to bridge the gaps between communities. It struck my fancy, too. So I took part in an event in Rockport. My sermon was entitled "The Faith We Live By." An old lady sitting in front of my wife, Ruth, said to her companion, "He's a rabbi; he must be Jewish."

I lived two years in Gloucester and made many inroads. I drew parallels and connections between religion and art for which I was commended in the local press. I spoke of the relevance of Judaism in the contemporary world. Even though, the Superintendent of Schools told me we Jews were there on " tolerance" only, we didn't belong, we were tolerated. I developed an approach for troubled souls, helped them accept their difficulties, not as an enemy but as a "study" partner, a *chaver*, implying that in the trouble lies the answer.

After leaving Gloucester, I accepted a position in Newburgh, New York, as close to *Gehinom* (purgatory) as one can be. Newburgh was the prime example of a "Conservative" congregation in a three-synagogue town. It was neither of the right nor of the left, neither Orthodox nor Reform nor of any

other distinct and recognizable ideology. It had vestiges of
both extremes and never found its own true identity. The leadership consisted of transplanted New Yorkers who saw the
synagogue as a local Jewish identity club, a monthly open
house where Jews mingled. Torah and its study was never
part of the agenda. One of my predecessors played into this
outlook. He used as his model Achashverosh (Ahashuerus),
the king in the Book of Esther. And the wine poured forth
kayn over as if it was endless, its source never drying up.

A young cantor was hired and he courted and married the
"pious one's" granddaughter. I wasn't invited to the wedding.
In fact, the "cantor" became, thanks to the "pious" grandfather, the source for all things Jewish in that congregation.

A Jewish shoemaker died in Newburgh. His son, his only
child, lived a bachelor's life in Washington, D.C. When I in-
terviewed his son for the eulogy, he stressed his father's hu-
mility. Immediately, the great sage, Yochanan ha-Sandlar
(Yochanan the shoemaker) came to mind. The deceased
shoemaker in his younger years spent daily time on the study
of Torah attempting to decipher the true meaning of Jewish
destiny. I met the shoemaker a few times, and he revealed
himself to me. Knowing what I did about him, I spoke of the
hidden "Thirty-Six Tzadiqim" (pious ones) that are in our
midst. Their honesty and sincerity are a balm for all of us.
Their energy sustains us spiritually, bearing out again the Jewish belief that it's the hidden ones who have tapped into the
ultimate power and healing that sustains this world. The son
was impressed by the eulogy and it was shared many times
among Jews elsewhere.

The greatest challenge in Newburgh came not from the
hidden agendas but from the ego-trips of some of its congregational leaders. As stated above, I didn't fit the role of the
country club Rabbi; rather, the hidden, the mysterious, waiting to be discovered was my cup of tea. All my life I've felt
there is a dark, hidden message within me. I tried to get to it
by every means and measure. Sometimes something would
emerge into consciousness, most times it sent psychosomatic

signals—pains that couldn't be traced to their source, outbursts stemming from deep inside of me, having the power of a "gusher."

During the Newburgh years, my late wife, Ruth, suffered from a variety of illnesses. She was under constant treatment. The doctors in many senses abandoned her. They didn't realize the depths of her illness and treated her with remedies that aggravated her condition. The president of the *shul* (synagogue) refused to recognize the gravity of her condition.

Around that time, we went to the New Jersey seashore for vacation. Ruth took sick and I was left with taking care of Rina. I was called back for a prosperous funeral. My eulogy was good and Seidman, the President, invited me for lunch. He fed me a non-kosher hot dog and then snitched on me. He gave Professor Artzt a list of ten particulars making me "unfit" to be a rabbi. My salary was withheld and a *beit din*, an ecclesiastical court, was convened. I was exonerated.

I lived in Newburgh for one and a half years. To me, it was a sentence of exile from life and I never felt I was serving a willing, warm, welcoming congregation.

From Newburgh, New York, we moved to Alexandria, Virginia. I was welcomed with open arms. Like my predecessor, I had been a student of Professor Mordecai Kaplan. My approach to Jewish life and lore was greatly influenced by him. Unfortunately, the honeymoon was short lived. I arrived in January 1956, and left in June 1957. During this short period, I became deeply involved in three issues, a) the nascent civil rights' movement; b) the emergence of Reform Judaism in Alexandria; and c) I began to sense Ruth's growing physical frailty. All of this impacted on my psyche. No matter what I said or did, no matter how successful or meaningful from a public stance it may have been, I sensed as if I were nothing. I saw myself as someone used.

The congregation being located in Virginia attracted "quick, shotgun marriages," young people hell-bent on escaping their parents' control over their lives who came to Alex-

andria seeking a marriage ceremony. Legally, one didn't have
to wait for the document—the moment one applied for a
marriage license; the document was immediately issued. A
clergy person said the words and the marriage ceremony took
place. When I was called to the congregation, I was told of
this bizarre practice and was expected to turn over *in toto* all
honoraria received by me. My *naïveté* in regards to the ways of
the world was fairly remarkable. I was anxious for employment and I accepted gratefully whatever was offered to me by
the congregation. An alcoholic *shamash* (sexton or beadle) sat
downstairs daily playing solitaire, and, in turn, would report
on my daily activities. He was the house spy and informant.
Nothing in the congregation interested me. Its ideology was
never discussed. Every evening a *minchah-ma'ariv* evening service was held and every Shabbat the usual quorum of ten appeared. The most pious among them was a European-born
retiree who read the Torah every week. He lived some distance from the synagogue and would arrive by public trans-
portation. His rational for Shabbat travel was strange to one
as myself, but in the end, he became one of my mentors.

An active Reform congregation flourished in Alexandria.
Its Rabbi was Emmet Franck (of three-hour conversion
fame). At one time, he was the assistant to Rabbi Gittelson of
Washington's Hebrew congregation. He emulated his former
Rabbi, forever seeking goodwill in the non-Jewish world. One
year, it was rumored, Rabbi Gittelson featured a Christmas
tree in his temple lobby. Rabbi Franck—believe it or not—
served an Easter ham at his public *seder* (Passover dinner)! Of
course, being who I am—discretion wasn't my act of valor—
I ridiculed the act and was therefore dubbed as a rabbi who
stirs up unnecessary controversy rather than a rabbi who
granted to all the right of their own personal expression. It's
only in hindsight that I sense the validity of this argument.
Jewish communities being what they are, where members of
every family have separate allegiances, a) belongs to a conservative congregation; b) to a Reform congregation; and c) says
"a plague on all your houses." I was caught in a maelstrom

leading to my resigning and moving elsewhere. Of course, the fact I took part in a panel discussion favoring civil rights for blacks didn't help in Alexandria, Virginia, in those days.

I had a few good moments during that short tenure. I delivered a eulogy at the leading Conservative Congregation in Washington, D.C, and was, for a few moments, a rising "rabbinic star."

From Alexandria, I moved to Bellaire, Texas. It's an extension of Houston, Texas. The day we arrived, newspapers proclaimed oil had been found in the municipal dump. Therefore, its populace need not be taxed for any municipal services. Many celebrated, many formed groups especially "refugees" from New York. Their philosophy was equal rights, equal communal obligations. They insisted the citizen, as a member of the collective whole, must share according to his ability for the "burden" of communal life. Wealth isn't an entrée to privilege, the thinking went. Texas being oil country, the land of the *nouveau riche*, the new class of sudden wealth resisted the thinking of the New Yorkers and other Easterners.

Our synagogue consisted of a small shack-like building. A pre-school group met there. The daily *minyan* (prayer quorum) was the leadership's preoccupation. Little effort was put into Shabbat or holiday programming. Somehow, the High Holidays—Rosh Hashanah and Yom Kippur—re-kindled whatever smoldering piety that lay dormant in these people's souls. They had a High Holiday choir. Sometimes there would be a *minyan*, at other times, not. My unraveling came when I joined a group of clergy to become a better hospital chaplain.

I was welcomed. One of the instructors, a Baptist, constantly discussed the "sinfulness" of homosexuality. Not crazy about this point-of-view, I nevertheless tried to get to know him. I visited his home, brought a gift for his newborn child (accompanied by Ruth). While there, I felt the need to confess to him that, as a young man at Yeshiva University and the Jewish Theological Seminary, I had experienced some fleeting (and, I later realized, quite common and normal) homoerotic encounters. This was a big deal—was Sky gay? What a scandal! At that time, there was no widely excepted notion that a predominantly heterosexual person could legitimately have some same-sex experiences. The minister moved for my expulsion. I didn't know what to do with it. The rest of the faculty was ready to help me, with the promise that I go into therapy. On a subconscious level, it was as if I sought diminution, perhaps a desire to be ostracized. I read Carl Jung. I wasn't fighting for any kind of gay rights; nevertheless, I followed their advice and found a psychiatrist.

This doctor was an odd duck. He himself had same-sex tendencies and had succumbed to his desires. He never attended to his professional business. He had lunch with me. He was always late for his appointment.

I left him and joined a group program. In this group was the temple president's daughter (with lesbian tendencies) and a gay man who had had oral sex with his son and had been with the group for four years. I flirted with him and he invited me to lunch. He picked me up at my apartment, (I'd moved out of congregation house hoping to leave the rabbinate and earn a psychology degree at the university). When I entered the car, he placed his hand on my thigh. I shirked and moved away. I asked to be let off.

I reported the incident to the psychiatrist leading the group. During a session, this guy denigrated God and himself. I quietly spoke up. He broke down and cried. He spoke at length about the goodness of his grandfather, how he wanted to be accepted by him, but instead, he sired a son and molested him. The psychiatrist said, "Harry caused a turnaround in the group."

Politics being what they are, my contract at the synagogue wasn't renewed, and I had to look for a job again. I met with Wolfe Kelman, the executive vice president of the Rabbinical Assembly, who was very fond of me and saw things in me I never acknowledged. In fact, through Wolfe I became aware how close I was to expulsion from the Jewish Theological Seminary. Someone on the faculty became aware of my tendencies and many (including in particular the famous Prof. Abraham Joshua Heschel, who unfortunately didn't like me very much) moved for my expulsion but Professor Arzt came to my rescue. Again, standing at the edge and yet not falling into the pot. He might have protested on my behalf: *Mah betza be-damai be-ridti be-shachat,* "What profit is there in my blood when I am descending into a pit?" (Psalms 30:10), perhaps to mean, "Hasn't Harry Sky suffered enough?" Wolfe Kelman had me always in mind. I think he suspected my proclivities.

This issue never caught up with me. I toyed with it in many ways even having deep feelings for some men. There is a homing device inside of me that keeps me from crashing. But the tendency of standing at the edge, at the precipice, almost slipping, has been there from childhood days. My fantasies, my seeking power through the energy of others, drives me on and on.

From Bellaire, I went to Beth El Zedek in Indianapolis. Wolfe had discussed me with some of the senior Rabbis. Aranson, Auger, Greenfeld, Waxman, Adler. I met with all of them and was chosen by Greenfeld. Here, too, I injured myself. I told Bill Greenfeld in a moment of anxiety and need for embracing and of pity, my past hurt, my proclivities. He warned me not to say anything to anyone. But I knew I'd dug my grave. As fate would have it, he took sick and I was left with the care of the congregation. My tenure was limited. At first, Bill Greenfeld had said he would send a letter to the congregation, urging them to consider me as a possible successor. He didn't and I, in my sloppiness, never marshaled the necessary support. I didn't prepare for our Talmud study sessions, nor did I handle the politics of the merging of our Hebrew school with the community school. I didn't prepare *bar mitzvah* students properly. Yet some felt I had a hidden greatness if only I would let it out. It showed itself in my politics always embracing, not pushing away in my eulogies and wedding addresses.

But I suffered from the old "gossip behind peoples' backs." It's still with me. My insecurity seems to hang on. When my Swiss psychiatrist and friend, Dr. Hermann Ströbel asked, "Who are you?" he was truly confronting the dilemma. The hidden one, the unborn one, Mashiach - the Messiah - among you.

Bill Greenfeld died. I was asked to serve as interim until a successor was elected. I shared my angst with others. In my political *naïveté*, they were poorly chosen. In fact, it stirred up some of the "elite" members thus sealing my fate. Julian, Bill's erstwhile partner, ran the congregation from the sidelines. He was disturbed by my politicking, called me into the office and said I had one year, with a $1,000 raise and that is it, start looking elsewhere. Buzya, Bill's widow, had some connections in Portland, Maine. She suggested I look into it. In those days, I seldom knew or responded to my inner self. If someone suggested something, it became a Divine message. I contacted Wolfe Kelman and he arranged for an interview.

"My first sermon title was 'Getting to know you.' It was well received. To this day, men and women who were in attendance remind me of its profound impact. I made it quite clear. I saw my rabbinate as a pilgrimage to peoples' hearts, minds, and souls."

ARRIVING IN MAINE

If truth be told, Portland's Beth El wasn't a prize position. If anything, it had the reputation of being a revolving door. In thirteen years of existence, four Rabbis served it: two for two years each, one for five years, and one for four years. Ephraim Bennett was everyone's hero. He laid the foundation for Beth El's future. Yet he knew and felt he was in a community with many versions of Jewish life. It wasn't a large community, perhaps two thousand families at its peak. In its favor was the founding group, Jews of public prominence and clout. The non-Jewish community considered them to be the best of the Jewish community. Whereas Shaarey Tphiloh, the Orthodox congregation, had a flavor of Eastern European *shtetl* about it, Beth El was the "American and modern" congregation. It had a first-class cantor and choir, accompanied by organ. Cantor Kurt Messerschmidt constantly strove for dignity and decorum at services. By the time I arrived, Beth El was thirteen years old. The history of Portland Jewry stretched back to *shtetl* days and traditions. It became a community in 1874 with the purchase of two house lots in South Portland for burial purposes. In 1904, Shaarei Tephiloh Synagogue was dedicated. It was on the bottom of Munjoy Hill, in the vicinity of the old Custom House.

The bulk of the Jewish community arrived after the Civil War (1864) and grew after the pogroms in the Russian Jewish pale. From 1874 to 1894 two major streams of immigrants arrived, one from Kurland, Latvia, in the vicinity of Riga, another from the Ukraine. Though the Kurlanders had been exposed to "modern, enlightened" thought, and tried as best they could to bring the reasoning of the Lithuanian, Latvian, and their Baltic-born Jews to Portland, the Ukranians brought with them the emotional drive of the *chasidim* (Chasidic Jews). Shaarei Tephiloh was built so that the various groupings and storefront synagogues could merge under one roof. The solidarity was short-lived. By 1906 or 1907 groups broke away.

Eventually one group left and built the "Cumberland Avenue" *shul* (synagogue) and another building was erected on Congress Street calling itself Etz Chaim, in memory of a Shaarei Tephiloh Rabbi, Chayim Shochet. Each building had its own enthusiasts and each was named and labeled by the "others." Cumberland Avenue people were derisively referred to as rag pickers, etc. Etz Chaim became the platform of the younger, liberal, anti-authority group.

In 1945 at the end of the Second World War, voices were raised asking for modernization. Sermons delivered in English began in the 1930s with the advent of Etz Chaim. A Sunday school was organized by Clarice Shur. The classes were held in the newly formed Jewish Community Center on Cumberland Avenue.

The Center itself had Norman Godfrey as its director. He was a follower of Mordecai Kaplan and accepted his doctrine of the need for a *qehilah*—an all-encompassing, all-embracing Jewish community. The selling point was its program. The JCC spoke to Jews who were not drawn to official institutions. By the time I arrived in Portland, JCC's priority in community programming was a given. It sported a theatre group, athletic programs, and inter-community programs for the adolescent and young adult Jewish community.

One day a delegation of JCC leaders came to see me and quite forcefully told me the parameters of community programs. What was JCC's domain and what was Temple Beth El's. Of course, I took umbrage and resisted. In time, we came to terms.

I've always considered myself a disciple of Prof. Mordecai Kaplan. He was my mentor, my reason for being a rabbi. He had restored to me my pride as a Jew. Through him, I was able to evolve a new theology; one that ultimately led me to the belief of the God within ourselves. Through him, I arrived at the unity of nature, of God, of the human, of all of us.

In the earliest years of my rabbinic career, I felt the call, the need to affirm "no Jew is more authentic than another."

It's what my congregations called for. Conservative Judaism is historical Judaism. Reform is radical Judaism. Orthodoxy was out of the modern mainstream. One of their leading spokesmen believed in *chadash asur min-ha-torah*—whatever is new or current is forbidden by the Torah.

I arrived officially on August 16, 1961. It was a Friday. I spoke at services. My first sermon title was "Getting to know you." It was well received. To this day, men and women who were in attendance remind me of its profound impact. I made it quite clear. I saw my rabbinate as a pilgrimage to peoples' hearts, minds, and souls.

My tenure truly began at the interview.

"Rabbi, will you attend daily *minyan*?" asked Tom Livingston.

I said, "If you will, so will I."

"Rabbi, what contract terms are you seeking?"

"Three years."

"Why?"

"The first, you'll love me," I assured them. "Second, you'll hate me, and in the third, we'll find a way to live with each other."

I viewed myself as the Rabbi of Temple Beth El, but also a spokesman for "faith and hope," for all who would listen. I didn't view myself as the Rabbi for Temple Beth El's members only. It was an uphill battle. Some congregants felt the place (the temple) was there to only serve their constituents. Several cleavages were extensive. At one point, Rabbi Bekritsky, the Orthodox Rabbi, cast aspersions on the Temple, its members and their Jewishness. Sometimes he said "members of the temple are not Jews." It seemed as if all of us—Jews—temple, and non-temple people were forever judging one another. In some instances, it seemed as if "A" shunned "B" because of an ancient hurt many generations ago.

Quite early in my Portland years, I realized my Rabbinate called for an approach different than that of my father and my ancestors. My father held on to the model of days gone

by. The Rabbi, first and foremost, was a talmudic scholar.
The text was foremost. A Rabbi is to be measured by his erudition. The American model was foreign to him and he held
it up to ridicule. The Rabbi as the pastor concerned with you
as a human cognizant of his own self was reminiscent of *minchag ha-goyim*, the non-Jewish approach to life. In his eyes,
peace of mind, a sense of duration in tune with one's self,
aware of psyche's needs bordered on witchcraft. To him,
God existed, but he was a distant owner, not a daily visitor
involved in your life, interested in it. In fact, one who spent
his/her time wondering about you and yours was an unwel-
comed busy-body. In one's early life (until the age of six) parents are expected to form and shape the young person's future. Thus, my deep dependency on my mother's ministrations was as normal as could be in my youngest years. I
sought solace from her. At six my father took over. From six
to twelve years of age, the rudiments of daily life are stressed.
The three r's of the secular world, and *tefilah* (prayer), *chagim*
(holy days), Jewish customs and procedures, *chumash* (the Pentateuch, with the interpretations of Rashi, Rabbi Shlomo
Yitzchaqi). *Mishnah* and the rudiments of Talmud study were
the basis of lifelong living and education for him. He didn't
join any congregation. He was a steady worshipper in a local
synagogue, the Tenth Street *shul* in Newark, N.J. There were
other synagogue models in Newark. My father distanced himself from them. He distanced himself from the usual routines
of American born, American raised boys. Baseball, football,
hockey, basketball were the activities of the idle. Good, tame,
practicing Jews sought constant opportunities for Jewish living and learning. In my father's eyes, the Rabbis and their
synagogues were incapable. The raising of good, upstanding
Jews who would assure the future of Jewish life called for different Jewish leaders. He harbored this feeling within himself
and conveyed it to all who would listen to him. He constantly
referred to the *shtetl* and its kind of Jews.

I'm convinced I absorbed these thoughts and feelings
even though I left home at the age of twelve when Pappa en-

rolled me in MTJ in New York City. There I acquired my *girsa de-yankusa*, my earliest memories and bits of Jewish "wisdom." For many years, I tried to reconcile the life I was living with the ideas he proposed.

Of course, my inner self resisted. My resistance spilled over into the realm of self-identity leading to much distorted adolescent behavior.

When I arrived in Portland, I somehow realized it was time to live my life not according to "Pappa" Yehudah Leib Sky, but Harry Z. Sky. Whenever I said, *ki hem chayeinu ve-oreikh yameinu* this is your life, the meaning and fullness of your life, a different ring emanated from those words. Not the life Pappa described with its *shtetl* memories but the life that would at last give me a feeling of arrival, of self-definition, of knowing who the "I" in my life existence is.

These 47 years in Maine were devoted to that idea. At first, my aggressiveness took over. I realized quite early that aggressive behavior is a mask. It attempts to mute one's rough spots. It tries to be the balm that soothes the turbulent waters. For me, those waters were kept alive by the presence of the Orthodox community. Rabbi Bekritsky was ordained at the Chafetz Chayim Yeshivah in Brooklyn, New York. To many, its ordinations were questionable. My father had a cousin who studied there and spent his entire life as an itinerant sometimes Rabbi, sometimes solicitor for orthodox institutions. He left a questionable taste in the families' mouths. Rabbi Bekritsky was more refined than "Cousin Simon." I quickly realized the limitations of Bekritsky's learning. He shunned comparative studies and the thought that Judaism and Christianity had an historical link. He was an upholder of the notion one must divorce oneself from any and all things that ring true to Christian notions.

I had accepted for myself Prof. Mordecai Kaplan's notion, "the *halakhah* has a vote but not a veto." The *halakhah* (Jewish tradition) was not set in stone. It, too, like any human institution is open to the rules of life. The sages of the Talmud taught, before legislating any issue or approach to one, *puq hazei* "go out and see what the people feel." How will they react, will it cause unnecessary hardship? I constantly sought means and measures of involvement, not separation. I never felt (since childhood) that Judaism's intent was to separate us from humankind. To me, the Jewish message is expressed in our prayer book, "The day will come when all will gather together on the mountain and affirm our belief, allegiance and devotion to the "one who spoke and the world came into being."

From childhood, life was overflowing with mysteries and unresolved questions and feelings. As I grew older, I realized religion, as we Jews understand it, was the attempt to help us live with the mysteries and perhaps arrive at solutions, especially solutions that provide us insight into what makes each one of us acknowledge our separate and collective rolls.

From my first day in Portland, I felt I was in the homeland of the mysteries. The forests, the lakes, the wooded areas, invited me and whispered to me its secrets. I was drawn to alternative answers. That is what the mysteries are about, whether it be *kabbalah*, Gnosticism, or alchemy. It's all alternative answers to life. One commentator said, "today the way to answer right wingers is to say, "I read the bible differently." Here's another answer. "I challenged constantly the established, the norm. On the first Shabbat morning service at Beth El, I refused to say everything in the normative *siddur* (prayerbook). A Mr. Simonds challenged me. I said, "What is this, *lokshen*-noodles? With *lokshen*, you eat every strand, not with *tefilah* (prayers)! The *siddur* (prayer book) is a compendium. Some things apply, others don't." He never came back to Temple Beth El. I didn't care. I stood my ground. They had a *minchag* (custom) to open the *aron* (ark) where the Torah is lodged when reciting the *Shema Yisrael*. I refused to do it, nor would I stand up for the *Shema*. In fact, in the ancient temple, it was recited seated.

My self-assertion took another turn. As mentioned before, my first sermon delivered on Friday evening, August 16, 1961 was entitled "Getting to Know You." As if to say in this stage of life, I was emerging from my cocoon; The butterfly testing its wings.

Up to that time, my entire life had been spent focusing on the question, "Am I alive?" Have I emerged from my mother's womb? Approximately twenty-five years later, in the course of an "active imagination exercise," I imaged the little one, whom I named "Harry It." I found him in a cave, a Mount Sinai cave. I knew "Harry It" was a neglected part of my "emerging soul or self" coming to "life." Am I awake? Have I emerged from my mother's womb or am I still attached to her? As I've stated earlier, many of my earliest memories and anxieties were played out in that endless circle of feeling neglected and abandoned. Whether in the preschool years when the family's energies seemed focused on my brother's health and viability or my inability to find the key for integration in the public school world, or the sense of strangeness and utter isolation in the yeshivah world, it was my father's, not my mother's, world. She wasn't a card carrying "*halachist*." I'm sure if she ever sat with other *halachist* followers of codes and norms, rabbis' wives, she would have felt out of place. Dressmakers, seamstresses, tailors, that was her cup of tea, not hair splitting Talmudists with their fine combing, fine tuning textual studies. My mother was the dreamer, unlike my father whose "field of dreams" was the Talmudic tales. Hers were peasant songs, tales told over and again. My mother took second place in the family hierarchy. Whenever my father was out of work, she filled in, even to the point of self-degradation. Both parents were passive-aggressive. My father had a heavy dose of unresolved adolescent macho feelings. His jokes were testosterone laden, usually couched in Hebrew textual innuendo. He was literate, my mother wasn't. She was a woman, a girl who never had formal schooling but had a deep native artistic feel about her.

I, on the other hand, sought relatedness yet never formed absolute attachments, to either person or idea.

Harold Pachios, a well known attorney who serve on many federal appointments, a partner of Senator George

Mitchell, as always, remarked on my openness, my willingness to talk to all. It was true, especially in the relations of non-Jews with Jews. There was always the pallor of acceptable or not. For years, I felt I was being watched: "Someone will tell a story about me, the strength of my Jewish observances, the boundaries of my Jewish allegiances." I feared someone might remember or have witnessed my angst in the arena of masculine identification. For if truth be told, at times I wanted to emulate my father, at times to be my mother's clone.

Relating to non-Jews began for me in the mixed neighborhoods of Newark. When I left Newark to study at the *yeshivot* (Talmudic academies), the relationship was stymied. The yeshiva world was a Jewish world. Its teachers, its masters, were forever seeking lapses in our behavior, lest we become like goyim, and live according to their customs. In Newark, especially during the early yeshiva days (1936 to 1939) when I studied at MTJ, my sights were not yet on texts and learning. MTJ was a form of exile. My father had arrived at the conclusion that the person he wanted me to be will never become that way in Newark's environment. "I" needed a new, a different venue. He'd regale me with his memories of Yeshieva days. At "Ladi," in Dvinsk, in the Ragatshover Bet Midrasch, etc. He never achieved his aim to be a Rav. He hoped against hope I would be. The Rav of which he spoke wasn't my dream. In fact, the overwhelming drive during those years of study was distancing myself from his dream for me. I acquired by osmosis "talmudic skills" not by studied design. By the time I reached Portland, I believe I'd worked through those questions and assumed the persona of a different kind of Rav than pappa's. My Rav was based on Kaplanian, Heschelian and other influences.

By the time I reached Portland, much had gelled within me, a new Harry Sky was emerging. It had gone through many steps. The rav image of pappa's youth; the rav image of *Torah ve-daat*; the rav image of JTS. All of this was tempered by my experiences in the field from Gloucester to Portland.

"When will America, and when will the rest of the world realize that true power is not military power but the power of the spirit? The power of the prophets that begs and urges, 'Come let us reason together! Let's put a lid on our fears and frustrations!' ... I began my address by saying, "What can we expect when the senior Senator of Maine is too busy with military affairs to find a few moments to discuss civil rights with clergy."

CIVIL RIGHTS

What I am today, my beliefs, my sympathies, my assertions, matured here in Portland, in Maine. I can truly say, I've shed the notion of "What will people say?" - Jews and non Jews alike. It is no longer the sole arbiter for my public statements and beliefs. Having sensed this feeling of release and relief, I embarked from my first day in Portland, on a "mission" of sharing my beliefs and understanding of life with others. It wasn't a calculated approach. It seemed to emerge.

One day, I met a colleague, the minister of the Methodist church on Forest Avenue. I sensed resistance on the part of many to my messages. He said, "You engage in too much of the prophetic thrust." I wondered what does it mean? It occurred to me my approach smacked of a bulldozer, "get out of the way or I'll flatten you on the spot. Hurry, hurry. If you don't share your message, your feelings, you have failed in your calling."

I somehow felt, for any society to succeed a level playing field has to be arrived at. Each of us is chosen in his/her own way. Since from birth we are discovering who we are, what is our calling, where do we fit into the great human experiment of *tiqun olam*—the repair of the fractured world. When the Methodist minister told me I had too much of the prophetic thrust, I didn't shirk my mission of *tiqun olam* as I understood it.

In the early days of my tenure, I was approached by the minister of the AME Church known as the Ethiopian Church. Throughout the U.S., muscles were being flexed and the call for civil rights was heard far and wide. He asked if I would join him in the "March on Washington." I had been at a Rabbinical Assembly convention and the forthcoming activities pertaining to civil rights was proclaimed in every leading newspaper in this country. I hesitated. I shared my questions and feelings with my congregants, the Friday Eve (*Shabbot*) after the convention. My hesitation was there, my fear was there. What would be the congregational response? I knew some of my congregants were raised in the metropolitan centers of these United States. I knew many Jews distanced themselves from the Black communities. After the service, Sumner Bernstein of blessed memory came forward and said, "Rabbi, go. We'll take care of all expenses incurred." He persisted. I was won over. I called my Black colleague and said, "Count me in." We became a team. He sent a telegram to Sen. Margaret Chase Smith asking for an audience. Her reply was short (not sweet). She is too busy with military issues to give time to us. We didn't meet. I met her in Washington on other issues but not on civil rights.

The meeting in Washington is as clear in my head these days as they were in those days (1963 to 1964). Martin Luther King, Jr. reminded me of Second Isaiah. A prophetic voice calling for justice rolling down as would a mountain stream. His hope for the world, a world in which his children will be able to play in an open and friendly way with others, white or Black, Christian or Jew—a day when no one will be forced because of his/her color to ride on the back of the bus. Ms. Parks would be allowed to sit in the front of the bus, with dignity, with hope, with acceptance. While sitting there, I turned around and suddenly I sensed a change in me. Whatever veil, whatever figment separated me from the "The Blacks" was gone. I saw them in their total human form. All I could think of was the speech in Shakespeare's *The Merchant of Venice*. "My eyes are like yours, my heart throbs as yours does." I was hooked. I returned to Maine with a deep resolve. Let's see what can be done here in our Portland. In those days, the Black community hadn't yet achieved its current prominent status. I was asked to speak at the AME Zion Church. My cadence changed. Many in the audience remarked that I spoke with the tone of the classic Black preacher. My 41-year-old son remembered the moment. Over and over again he would ask me to speak that way again. I joined the NAACP and became active in its local chapter. I befriended Jerry Talbot. Rev. Thompson of Woodford's

Congregational Church and I helped Jerry. We found him employment and encouraged him in his quest for true equality. Those were heady days. In fact, when the horror of the Birmingham Four occurred (four Black girls were killed in the bombing of a Black church in Birmingham, Alabama), a public protest was organized. Rabbi Bekritsky, Portland's Orthodox Rabbi, and I marched in the front line of the parade. I was asked by my fellow clergy to deliver the address. I did so. My heart cried out for these innocent victims. I was angry. When will America, and when will the rest of the world realize that true power is not military power but the power of the spirit? The power of the prophets that begs and urges, "Come let us reason together! Let's put a lid on our fears and frustrations!" They said, "Not by power, not by might says *Adonai* (God), but by my spirit." We all have *Adonai's* spark within us, let that be the guiding force in human affairs. I began my address by saying, "What can we expect when the senior Senator of Maine is too busy with military affairs to find a few moments to discuss civil rights with clergy."

I could hear the intake of breath in the audience. A newspaper reporter asked for a copy of my address. I handed it to him. A few days later an emissary from Senator Smith tracked me down and said she wanted me to apologize. I replied that I'm one of her constituents just as you are. Let her approach me directly. She never did. But a few months later, when Vietnam was on Page One, we had a rally of clergy at Temple Beth El and we adopted a resolution questioning the wisdom of our Vietnam policy. I was informed that a piece of literature, emanating from the Senator's office was accusing me of being a "Communist." So it goes. That's the price for being too much of the "prophetic thrust."

There were other sideshows. A Methodist bishop said in South Portland that Blacks weren't deserving of civil rights, "They are the descendents of Ham, the son of Noah of biblical infamy." It smacked of the post Auschwitz comment, "The Jews deserved extinction. They were guilty of Christ's death."

Vietnam brought great anxiety to all of us who had concluded arms, missiles weren't the answers humans sought. Some of us when approached by young people of military age, said, "Take a leave of absence, go live elsewhere. For this too shall pass. It is inequitable. It is unjust." "Be still," Moses told his contemporaries. We said the same thing. "Be still, be scarce." Fortunately our venue was America. We were at the edge of being a police state but not there yet.

National security in those days (the 1960s) was the catchall, a justification for all things (unfortunately, similar to our times with the Second Gulf War and Iraq). Under the national security umbrella, all sorts of things were tucked away. Films emanating from Hollywood showed us the ludicrousness of this title—scandals, payoffs, doctored ledgers.

The 60s were civil rights days - for Blacks, for the handicapped, for the elderly, for Jews, for union groups, for women. I felt drawn to all of these causes. They were symptomatic of America's shortcomings. Some are privileged; others are there to serve them. It was what was later termed the "trickledown theory." It was the hue and cry of the "born-again"-ers. God listens to us; the rest are paving their own way to Hell.

It reminded me of what the Superintendent of Schools said to me in Gloucester, "Jews are here on tolerance. You had better accept that or face the trials of life." I have refused to be taken in by such thinking. My metaphor was the Biblical one that said, the first human was the prototype of all to follow. Whatever emerged on the human scene stemmed from it. No gradation, no privileges. Just be human or as it was said in Yiddish, "Sei a mensch" (behave as a decent human being should behave).

Armed with this truth, I scanned the world around me. I sensed the message I was carrying. The Jewish message emphasized this idea. 1) Sei a mensch, 2) make sure the playing field was level so everyone would be comfortable with the measure of menschlichkeit. For me, it began in everyone's own backyard. Proverbs taught to teach the young one on his own level, on his own playing field. Don't impose standards beyond his understanding. Don't expect the young person who isn't physically coordinated to be a first-class athlete. Don't say to the young man or woman, "Follow in your parents' footsteps. They were artisans, so should you be. They were lawyers, doctors; therefore that is your profession too. Listen, listen, listen, and once you hear the true tones of your soul, let that be the springboard of your life. Moreover, become aware of your child's destiny, his or her destiny may differ from yourd. Accept it with grace and loving kindness." I knew this to be the truth, called for by our times. This was especially true in the realm of Spirit and faith.

I've devoted my life to this premise. It's my coming to terms with the life I knew and with which I grew up. As I stated earlier, I found myself in Maine, in Portland, in Falmouth. Until I arrived in Maine, I was literally speaking the wondering one, perhaps the legendary wondering Jew. Gloucester, Mass., Newburgh, New York, Alexandria, Virginia, Belaire, Texas, Indianapolis, Indiana were my venues. In each, I caught a glimpse of the unborn me. In Maine I gave birth to all that was potentially me.

"If we are to survive as a people and a tradition, we have to take to heart our communal mission. Every person has within him or herself an internal mission. It's part of their life journey. We become aware of it early in life. We also realize as humans, we can't go alone. We cannot achieve a sense of fulfillment, personal or communal, in isolation."

IDENTITY

One of the earliest issues in my life was the issue of identity. Who am I, what am I, what was my destiny in life. The last question was resolved during a private moment in my mid teens. I knew I was destined to be a Rabbi - a teacher of inner truths. But first I had to find my own inner truths. I knew quite early in life the wonderful *midrash* taught by the ancient sages. God is unlike other creators. They create a mold (or a print) and copies are made. God, in creating the human, instills his breath in the individual. Every human contains that creative God spark within themselves. Thus, the human created in God's image has the power to create, to discover, to mold, to fashion and to change. Having this power, the human tries to put it to good use. But, unfortunately, there has always been a class of people in all classes, in all groups, in all nations, who impede the creative process. Rabbi Moshe Sofer said, "All new ideas, all new inventions are forbidden by the torah." Thank goodness, many differed with him and the creative spark within the human community has continued in its path of creation.

New cures for incurable diseases, new materials, stronger, lighter, of greater pliability have appeared on the human scene. Oftentimes, though, these new creations are usurped by governments, military communities and others and are reserved for "defense purposes" (read "conquering of enemies", suspected and proven and a storm of honor and destruction rains down upon us and innocent bystanders.

The misuse of the new, the usurpation of the creative process, the channeling of its vitality into military "protective channels" has often times interfered with the natural development of the human species.

The principle and the debate over which wars are obligatory and which are discretionary has been with us since the Talmudic period. The principle of *Milchmet Chov* (obligatory wars) and *Chov* (discretionary wars) has been applied to these areas of human conduct. For example, in the realm of prayer, the Mishnah Berakhot, states in the evening, the two blessings preceding the recitation of the *Shema* (hear or listen, o Israel or fellow Jew. *Adonai* is our God, *Adonai* alone) and the blessing after the *Shema* introducing the *Amidah*, the silent prayers are obligatory.

In other areas of life, the sages said this is obligatory, this is voluntary. It wasn't a unanimous opinion, one that was without question. Everything was debated in the pages of the Talmud. For we Jews always felt and believed God is in a state of becoming and revealing. As God is, so are we humans. For we are and have always been in His image. We sensed God's frustration with the human. We realized God's ultimate decision (of Genesis). The human is not a perfect being. In one sense, whatever he/she is has always been the same. The image is the rainbow. The human on every level, in every situation is in a state of revelation, in a state of becoming, moving from one shade of the rainbow to another.

Jesse Jackson understood this thesis when he spoke of Black-White relationships. Scientists in laboratories and at conferences promulgated this notion when they spoke of the telling point in each substance. It is the very essence of human existence. We are in a constant state of becoming and discovering.

When I arrived in Portland on August 16, 1961, I faced a congregation that seemed to be in a dormant yet budding state. It was at that time 13 years old. During that period, four Rabbis had served it. Many wondered how long my tenure would be. I was told three or four years after my arrival, a wager was made in a betting parlor. Some said I'd survive six months, others said one year. One said more than two years, and he won the bet. He invited me to breakfast and revealed the incident. I looked at him and smiled. I asked, "How much did you win? So where is my cut?" his response, "Rabbi, this breakfast is on me."

It seemed to many that I was a bag of surprises, never knowing completely where I was headed. Neither did I know.

But this much I realized. Like God, wherever and whomever He may be, I was in a state of becoming, a revelation. In years gone by, this telling fact provoked frustration. Congregants accustomed to a well thought out and focused life were frustrated by my behavior pattern. "Rabbi," they would say, "yesterday or the day before, you said thus and thus, today you are arguing another point of view. Where is your consistency?" As I grew older, I found an answer. I said God in talmudic terms is known as *Hamakom* - the place of the consistent one. But Moses said to God (as did Abraham and others), "what if" and God relented. The great "what-if" the Talmud solved by saying *bari ve-sheima bari adif*—"between a certainty and a mere possibility, the certainty prevails" (Talmud Bava Metzia 116b). My life was a constant *sheima*, a constant "what-if." I always sensed in my case and in another's situation, we don't know the whole story. Something is waiting in the wings, ready to be born.

In August 1961, I called a meeting of the Temple's (Beth El) ritual committee. I raised a question. Our sons and daughters are subject to the same Hebrew school curricula yet when they enter their 12-13 year, the year of *mitzvoth* (tradition teaches we possess in Judaism 613 commandments), of accepting (in at least an adolescent way), the commitments of Jewish life, separate ceremonies are held for boys, separate ceremonies for girls. My oldest child, Rina, was nine years old and my wife, Ruth, of blessed memory, and I wondered, what will be her Bar Mitzvah ceremony. I was fortunate in having as my cantorial colleague, Kurt Messerschmidt, a man of great talent and of deep spiritual commitments. During his tenure, (he arrived at Beth El in 1951), the girls became *b'not mitzvah* (daughters of the commandments) on the festival of *Shavuot* (at the traditional and ancient anniversary of the giving of the Torah and commandments at Mt. Sinai, seven weeks after Passover). It was a group venture. The young ladies wore white choral gowns, and for many, it became the "coming out" party of early adolescence. In my enthusiasm, I remembered the tradition at Beth El Zedek, my Indianapolis congregation. Their working premise was complete equality in Synagogue life for men and women. Women counted in the choir, in the quorum (*minyan*), norm, in being officers of the congregation. My senior Rabbi, William Greenfeld, of blessed memory, had been deeply influenced by Mordecai Kaplan and so was I. Kaplan's daughter was the first *Bat Mitzvah* in American Jewish life. Until then only boys had celebrated the ceremony.

The meeting was convened. I made my case, and it was unanimously adopted. Three of the upcoming *b'not mitzvah* families demurred, left our congregation and joined Shaarei Tefilah, the Orthodox synagogue.

In those days, Shaarei Tefilah's leadership questioned our (Beth El) Jewish credentials. Their Rabbi, Morris Bekritsky, believed all innovations are forbidden by the Torah. He refused to acknowledge my ordination as a Rabbi. The Jewish Theological Seminary, my alma mater, was a hotbed of heresy in his eyes. When it was discovered that my undergraduate degree was issued by Yeshiva University, I automatically became a heretic in Rabbi Bekritsky's eyes. I wasn't phased by his barbs and innuendos. I believed in God as I saw Him. Rabbi Bekritsky saw God as he knew Him. Rabbi Bekritsky's great dream was to return to the values of the Eastern European *shtetl*. Mine was the ultimate bridging of disparate groups within the human world. Hitler's policy of a "judenrein", a Jewish-free Europe or, for that matter, world, found its counterpart, as far as I was concerned, in orthodoxy's insistence, only their kind of Jew is a legitimate Jew. I said then and say now, once you indulge in "chosen-ness," you are treading a dangerous road. I hailed Professor Mordecai Kaplan for his courage. He refused to accept any standard of "chosen-ness". In his prayer book, God is praised for having brought us (humans) close to Him, allowing us to catch a glimpse of His infinity and eternity. He said, "*Kdoshim* (be consecrated unto me) is holiness, not separateness."

We can all become "*Kdoshim*" holy, distinct, spiritualized human beings of whom the psalmist spoke when he asked,

"Why are we humans a little lower than the angels, the messengers, the God infused ones?"

This insistence on separateness has led to estrangement and unnecessary barriers of fear and suspicion. Our generation calls for bridges, not "chosen-ness." If the great spiritual teachers are correct in their definitions, then it is our human task to seek out the hidden, the unique in ourselves and in others and let our uniqueness be the pillar of smoke by day and the fire by night which legend tells us was the guide that led the ancient Israelites through the wilderness on the way to the Promised Land.

Somehow in Maine, I felt such beacons and pillars are in abundance. One could always find a fresh, new voice chirping. "Follow me. I'll bring you to the destined shores and places." Once we established the new traditions each young lady, the bat mitzvah, like her brother, the bar mitzvah was awarded her public moment. Cantor Messerschmidt continued, in his most dignified and learned way, to prepare these young people for their sacred public moment. We continued with our egalitarian program. A woman was elected president of our congregation. Cantor Messerschmidt continued his unmatched cantorial and choral work. Our youth and adult choir both attracted talented voices and our sacred services were known throughout the ranks of our Synagogue movement.

I realized quite early in my Maine Rabbinic career that we have entered into a new period in Jewish life. If we are to survive as a people and a tradition, we have to take to heart our communal mission. Every person has within him or herself an external mission. It's part of their life journey. It is prompted by their internal mission. We become aware of it early in life. We also realize as humans, we can't go alone. We cannot achieve a sense of fulfillment, personal or communal, in isolation.

I am a student of the Swiss Psychoanalyst, Dr. Carl G. Jung. I've learned much from him and his disciples. He fathomed the human as an outer and inner being. The human lives in the day-to-day, contemporary world, simultaneously carrying within himself the collective wisdom of generations gone by. Each of us possesses a sense of self that defines who we truly are and can potentially become. Jung's theories answered many questions for me. It helped me understand the world as I saw and experienced it, including my inner world, the world that is me.

My early upbringing hinted at a notion which saw the human as a compromised being. He's filled with needs, desires, and ambitions. More often than not, they become the engineers that drive his life vehicle and chariot. In Jewish tradition, a very articulate school insisted these personal drives, allowed to be the force in a person's life leads to "unacceptable behavior." The pious one mutes his drives. The *musar* (pietistic) movement was built on these premises. I had tasted the *musar* approach when I studied at *Torah V'daat* in Brooklyn, New York, a traditional *yeshiva* based on *musar* and *Chassidic* principles. The "Mussarniks," acting from the strength of their convictions, enticed many young people to their approach. It expressed itself in extreme acts of observance. The *Chofets Chayim* like other great authors, renown by their seminal publications, wrote a code of his own, the *Mishna Brurah*. His approach to study and observance was crystal clear in its insistence that the slightest divergence or compromise in Jewish observance leads one to the very gates of perdition (*gehenna* or *scheol* or oblivion). It applied to personal relationships, familial relationships, business dealings, etc. In regards to the Sabbath and festival observations, one must distance oneself from any act or thought that may lead to the breakdown of the fences that separate the observant from the compromisers. The *musar*-niks and other groups within the traditional Jewish camp took issue with my *alma mater*, the Jewish Theological Seminary, its rabbinic organization, the Rabbinical Assembly, and at a public ceremony placed a ban on us. In 1954/55 I received a letter from *Torah Vodaat* soliciting funds. I wrote them, "Since I was in a state of *cheirem* (excommunication), tradition forbids you to communicate with me either personally or through messengers. The postal service is your messenger, why do you ignore your ban?" They answered, "*Kesef mumar, mutar*, the funds, the possessions of a heretic can be used for sacred purposes (i.e., the support of their institution). I said, "*Cheirem* works both ways. I'm banned in your eyes; you are in mine."

When I arrived in Portland, I sensed a chasm dividing the Jewish community. Shaarei Tephiloh represented the orthodox, the traditional element—Temple Beth El, the non-Orthodox. Under non-Orthodox one found Jews who questioned the authority of Jewish Law. Many of us felt all of life was a product of evolving situations. We felt the concept of all of Jewish law was presented to us at one moment in time, fanciful.

To me and some of my colleagues, "Jewish law," and all other aspects of Jewish living is a continuously evolving process. This seems to be nature's way. To us it means this is God's way. Many have accused the Hebrew bible as being inconsistent. One thought is expressed in one place, its opposite in another. Many times, I was accused of inconsistency. Inconsistency isn't a shortcoming in human behavior or thinking.

Two students once approached the illustrious Abraham Joshua Heschel in the corridor of the Jewish Theological seminary. One of them asked him a question and he replied. Next day the second student met Prof. Heschel. He posed the same question. Heschel gave a contradictory answer. "But, Professor, yesterday what you said contradicts the current statement." Heschel answered, "that was yesterday. Bovines are constant, not humans."

Consistency has been the claim of all orthodox and authoritarian approaches to life. President George W. Bush flaunted his "consistency" from the moment he ascended the presidential "throne." "One must stand strong, one must uphold the traditions of the past," says he. We who see life as a process, God as process, see all of existence in a state of becoming. We welcome change, inconsistency, new frontiers, removal of barriers and realize within the human lies the solution to all of his concerns and disgruntlements.

Prof. Kaplan once said in class, "The modern Jewish heresy is the Shulchan Aruch," the consistent code of Jewish Law. God, in a state of becoming, can never be presented in final form, nor can God's revelation be of one moment only.

When I arrived in Portland, the Jewish community consisted of two different groups, the orthodox (*Shaarei Tefila Etz Chayim*) and the non-orthodox (*Temple Beth El*). I took it upon myself to help articulate the differences. I had my detractors. There were many who felt the differences must be bridged. I knew, both consciously and unconsciously, this was an almost impossible task. Non-orthodox meant what it said. None of us are in a perfect, completely fulfilled state. Many of us, colleagues and lay members of our communities, were being daily exposed to the new form of thinking (Freudian, Jungian, etc.) that sought to delve deeper and deeper into our respective psyches and untangle the various threads of our personalities.

We continuously ask, "Who am I? What is my destiny? Why am I here? What is my place in the great Jewish mystical undertaking of *tiqun olam*—the repair of this fractured world?" Every few months another crack in the fractured world appears. The 60's exposed many fissures. Some were in the body politic; some were in the realm of religious/spiritual life. Some pointed to gaps in democratic acceptance. Only members of one class or another, only males, only physically able, only young and non-retired personnel.

My agenda was clear. If our tradition was as Isaiah said, "A light unto the nations," the need for repair within our own ranks was being revealed.

As I stated above, the first act was the reshaping of the Bar/Bat Mitzvah ceremony. Second, granting to women full membership in the "minyan," the quorum for religious services. With the broadening of acceptance, the sisterhood took on greater roles in the life of the congregation.

The USY (The United Synagogue Youth) expanded and more and more of our youth participated in the USY annual pilgrimages to Israel. Our young people were exposed to a phenomenon not realized in the USA. Many Israelis felt and believed only one road was open to the "believing Jew" – the way of the *dati* – "authentic, traditional Jewish living and belief." Some, in more recent times, have been exposed to the thinking of the Hartman Institute and others who have placed Jewish beliefs, customs, and activities within the context and time period in which they surfaced. In other words, very little can be considered external never having evolved.

One day, Rabbi Berent, of blessed memory, and I met in Rabbi Bekritsky's study. We were considering the situation of *kashrut* (dietary laws) in Portland. He tried to place the blame for the weak situation on us (the non-Orthodox). I responded and said the question isn't the community but the personnel brought into town. He quickly changed the subject, pulled out a Temple Beth El bulletin and confronted me with it. I had proposed if we want to understand the period of the Mishnah (the early rabbinic period from second-century B.C.E. to second-century C.E.) we must consider the New Testament. Both Paul and Jesus asserted and affirmed their Jewishness and in the early days of the Christian community, their writings were seen as the product of another Jewish sect. Rabbi Bekritsky was incensed. I said, "Rabbi, I'm happy you are on our mailing list and are aware of our courses. You are welcome to attend, even differ in class, but the power of censorship is not in your hands. For us, authority in Judaism goes beyond the "Orthodox."

To us, the ever-evolving tradition was central. It became the impetus of my life. For I felt personally something was calling from within me as if it were saying, "Let me out, let me out."

"Being a student of Jewish tradition, I asked myself the question, if it was the creator's intention for us humans to be forever separate from one another, then why is the Creation story, the story of one human?"

ISRAEL

As early as 1947, I entered into psychoanalytic analysis. My analyst was Dr. Eva Rothman, a fascinating, erudite woman. She had an M.D. from Berlin, and a series of Ph.D's in child psychology, in art and drama and other fields. A friend of mine, aware of my own inner angst, suggested I see her. I worked with her throughout my seminary tenure. She helped me in many ways. She opened for me the window which "let the sun shine in." Through her and my JTS professors, I was able to accept the notion of "becoming" on a personal, communal, and universal level. Our discussions ranged far and wide: psychology, philosophy, mythology, the current political scene. With her keys and her eyes, I was able to view the world from a much wider perspective. Thanks to her, I realized the hidden purposes of traditional agendas. "Namely, if you ventured beyond the boundaries of the *daled amot* (cubits, limits) of the *halakhah* (formal codes), the proscribed boundaries of Jewish thought, law and custom, you endangered its survival." In time this seemed to be a weak reason for tradition. Through dream analysis and other associative forms of thinking, I managed to remove slowly but surely the many layers of protection that held me back from the wider world. In time, I discovered the Jewish quest for "security" – theological, mythical, philosophical, psychological – was universal. Non-Jews were as committed to defending their turfs as we were in defending ours.

1961 was 16 years after the cessation of European and Pacific hostilities. In the meantime, the Korean escapade came and went. Vietnam was heating up. Israel had been declared a State and admitted into the ranks of the U.N., though not with grace. The old undercurrents that sought the demise of an independent Jewish theological-philosophical existence still had its proponents. From the demons of the Holocaust to the Neo-Nazis who sought to end the battle once and for all times, we Jews were forever on the alert. In our desire and need for self defense, we sometimes became passive aggressive combatants. 1961 was a turning point in the age-old battle for human rights. I placed myself in the middle of the battle arena.

The 60's were heady years. Wherever we turned, we sensed stretching of mind, body, and spirit. To stretch our minds, experimental psychologists introduced drugs. One day someone called me and suggested I look into the possibility of mind stretching. He offered to take me to a session of "transcendentalists." I was aware of the transcendentalists of the 19th century. How did they differ from the 20th century version? Drugs. Drugs changed the experimenter in many ways. Some participants in this "sport" imagined themselves walking on walls and ceilings. Writers felt barriers were melting. The unacceptable of yesterday was the acceptable of today. In every field, every realm of human activity, as one observed the drugged state, one noticed changed facial features. Voices changed and taboos fell by the wayside. One of my friends participated in a drug experiment at the University of Houston. His antics were recorded and we, his friends, viewed the video. Many of us felt the predictions of Buck Rogers had come to life. We wondered what happened to the one we knew. Many of the participants in the drug experiments seemed to have crossed the Rubicon; physically and spiritually.

I was intrigued by this new knowledge. It seemed to speak to me. It pointed the way to go beyond limitations. Transcendence occurs in many ways. There is a transcendence of social barriers but, in many cases, the "drugs" were the pathway to transcendencies beyond the acceptable in human circles.

I was once called by a parent to counsel her son. He refused to eat the vegetables prepared for the family meal. He insisted his food be taken from the ground and immediately eaten. When he sat down to eat, his entire complexion changed and if one looked closely, one sensed he'd gone into another state of being. That, too, is transcendence. In the realm of sexual behavior, drugs were used to enhance and exaggerate all feelings involved in sexual moments from the size of body parts, to the sensation one felt when the epidermis was touched. The market place joined the transcendentalists. Some of these drugs were added in "safe form," thus enhancing whatever the product may have been. It is as if we cannot accept who we are and what has been "us" from our birthday. Enhance, betterment, forever going beyond who you are.

In realizing this tendency, I was challenged by the teaching of our Jewish tradition. Who is wealthy? He who accepts who he is and what he is and doesn't attempt to be someone else.

In the mid sixties, a few Jewish grandmothers spoke to me. Their grandchildren had been born in a "Christian denomination" hospital. One of the devoted religious nurses had baptized their grandchildren before bringing them to their Jewish birth mother. They were disturbed by this action. I tried to placate them. I said, "In God's eyes, the child will be regarded by the life he lives, not the baptism he received." It was a Jewish position. I spoke to Bishop Feeny about these incidents and he ruled no child shall be baptized without his parents' consent.

A few years later, I served as President of our Ministerial Association. My Christian colleagues bemoaned the fact that some clergy refused to join our union. Trying to enroll the Roman Catholic Clergy, I met with Bishop Feeny. At first, he refused to engage in this bit of interdenominational activity. Later, he reneged and the gates were open. Catholic clergy joined the Ministerial Association. Every day brought another crack in the walls separating us humans from each other.

Philosophically I pondered the question of human separateness. Being a student of Jewish tradition, I asked myself the question, if it was the creator's intention for us humans to be forever separate from one another, then why is the Creation story, the story of one human? Why is the animal and plant world replete with innumerable species? Yet among us humans, oneness seems to predominate. We seem to have the same systems that in the aggregate spells human. Is this by accident or by design? Secondly, is the oneness so distinct? We have variations within the human species; size, skin color, tolerance of differences, ability to cope with life's variables. If we study the "living" situation of humans, all seek shelter, clothing, and food. All possess sexual and other drives. And, yet, we seem to be at constant loggerheads with each other. Why? I've studied one system after another seeking answers. I participated in one program after another thinking "Here lies the answer." If only we humans would act in one or two or three fashions, changes would surface, new beliefs would take over. At times, I felt guidance must come from above. Life is a pyramid with an enormous base, narrowing to a miniscule apex. I believed governments and societies are the telling group. But then I was reminded of the phrase in psalms, "Don't rely on princes and those who hold the reins of power." The text says they can't help you. For they, too, are subject to the rules of nature and life. The immortality they claim is but "a passing dream," a whiff and a puff.

I felt the need in 1967, the period of the Six Day War in Israel, to seek a deeper source of strength and dependency. On July 1,1967, I flew to Israel. I rented a room in Tel Aviv and went with my official introductory papers to various departments seeking interviews and understanding. When I arrived in Jerusalem, I checked into a hotel room, quickly made my way to the Wall, the Kotel. Many claims are made for this wall. Its stone blocks are from the Herodian period - the second temple period. When I arrived in'67, the rubble hadn't been cleared. During the Jordanian occupation of the old city, the area surrounding the Wall was used by them as a garbage dump. All the dirt and filth of the city was thrown there. An unbearable odor surrounded the place. It reminded me of one of the predictions of Jeremiah pertaining to the fate of the first temple in Jerusalem. I walked up and down the length and breadth of the Wall. I found a quiet, secluded spot. I quickly doffed my *talit* (prayer shawl) and *tefilin* (phylacteries) and wailed, literally wailed. All of my pain, sorrow, uncertainty, and wonder of why do the wicked prosper, found an outcry in that wrenching wail. "God, God," I screamed, "Where are you? Answer me, please answer me. I believe in you, believe in me!"

I experienced an epiphany. I saw in my mind's eye, "the seeing eye" of the mystics. For a moment, I sensed Ezekiel's creation of the four expressions. I read, I saw, I sensed all that I had ever read of the many faces of God. It all was there, and I saw the many faces of my own fate; my wife's illness, my brother's frailty, my confused, inner identity. It was there. I was robed in sacred garments and straps, yet my inner self said, "No, there is a deeper meaning to my life." In that primal scream, I had broken through the barriers of daily existence and penetrated the taboo chambers of the "world above." I stood at that spot for approximately three hours. My lips moved. I was like Hannah of the Eli story. My lips moved as did hers. She wasn't intoxicated nor was I. She opened her heart and all of the pent up pressure poured out. Her plea was acknowledged. I think I, too, received an answer. The answer was *lo ba-shamayim hi*—"What you seek isn't in heaven but within yourself."

The years since the '67 trip were checkpoints for the message, "It's in you." From '67 onward, I visited Israel annually. In '73, the entire family spent one month there. During that time, I enrolled in a Hebrew University course on the archeology of Jerusalem. I noticed then, as I've noticed at other times, my innate ability to win over people, not through an abundance of facts, statistics and ideas but, rather, through a thought that passed through my head. Such moments brought me invitations to speak, to share and oftentimes gave me a glimmer of hope, a feeling of "This is it. This is the moment I've searched for. It's nebulous, it's seldom completely defined."

One day I dreamt a dream. I was standing at the entrance to a long, dark corridor. Somehow I knew on its left side, the corridor housed stables for sturdy horses, the kind that led the chariots for Roman government and military adventures.

At the end of the corridor, a light shone, it could have been a light bulb (artificial light) or sunlight. I walked into the corridor holding onto a railing on its right side. I could hear the horses on the left side stirring. I was tense, unsure, wondering if the stallions will break through. I walked and walked, every so often checking my feelings. At last, I was a few feet away from the end of the corridor, and I knew I possessed the "strength" to face the impending horror, fear, insecurity that is my life. "Even galloping horses won't destroy me." This good feeling endured for a short period of time, but the old insecurities arose. Time and again, they came back to my identity questions, referring to my Jewishness, my masculinity, my concern about the future.

"I feel that part of my life is being driven by its own energy. My siblings and my wives are deceased. I live alone in a retirement facility in Falmouth, Maine. Yet, I know I am still in the state of becoming."

FAMILY

I met my first wife, Ruth, in 1949. I had gone to a Zionist young adult camp in New Hampshire called *"Tel Noar".* Many of us Jewish Theological Seminary students went there. After a week I was bored. So I told my friend that I was going home. He said, "Don't go. There's a woman coming today, Ruth Levinson. She's for you." So I started walking back to my bunk. And there, unannounced, sitting next to my bunk was this woman. I sat down, struck up a conversation with her, and before I knew it I had asked her out and she accepted. I was so struck with her that I proposed to her two days after we met. A month later she accepted.

We were married in December of 1950. My daughter was born in August of 1952. For the first six months we rented part of one of these New York townhouses on 85th Street near Central Park West. It was a nice place but very crowded, everything was in one room.

The first six months of our marriage were heavenly, blissful, filled with dreams for the future. Most of my days and nights were devoted to preparation for my "final exams." While studying at the Seminary I taught Hebrew and other Jewish subjects of pre-Bar Mitzvah students. On Sundays my wife Ruth assisted me. Whatever monies we earned together was devoted to our living expenses. Entertainment in those days consisted of weekly trek from 85th Street and Central Park West to Broadway and 72nd Street. On that corner stood the Newsreel Theater.

I was ordained June 1951. My first pulpit was Gloucester, Mass, followed by short periods in three separate congregations ending up in Portland, Maine, August 16th 1961. The big thrill for us was "Saturday night" walking down Broadway, 72nd Street, where there was a newsreel theater on Broadway and 72nd Street. We'd stop at every store and look inside and say "When we have some money, I'm going to buy this and when we have some money I'm going to buy that."

Those were the days when television just began, so for 25 cents, we'd go into the Newsreel Theater, we'd watch the newsreel, and we went downstairs into the basement and we'd see Sid Caesar, the Israel program. Between the newsreel and the Sid Caesar program it was like a three-hour show. Then we walked back up Columbus Avenue. And every single Saturday night we'd buy ourselves a big piece of cheesecake at Delmonico's and have it for breakfast the next morning.

During my first decade in Maine, in Portland, our family grew. My youngest son, Ari, was born in 1963. He was named for my recently deceased father. His siblings were Rina, born in 1952 in Gloucester, and, Uri, born in 1959 in Indianapolis. Each of my children has their own distinct personality. All three are married and each sired a son and a daughter. I believe all three of my children have at least found themselves and are working in their chosen fields.

I feel that part of my life is being driven by its own energy. My siblings and my wives are deceased. I live alone in a retirement facility in Falmouth, Maine. Yet, I know I am still in the state of becoming. My inner wheels are forever in motion, and I haven't as yet experienced the ultimate Aha! I am still the traveler seeking a bit of "nirvana" for himself. Each day I get a glimpse of it, but like Moses of old, I'm privy to only a bit of it. Being a proponent of "We are in a state of becoming" point of view, nothing surprises me. I don't believe in accidents. I do believe whatever passes me or crosses my path is not of today or yesterday. It had to happen. It is a serendipitous moment.

My children (all three of them) felt their lives were being lived in a fish bowl. Being the Rabbi's children was a heavy burden. Each, in his/her own way, tried to come to terms with this reality. My daughter found comfort in her teen years in the company of other clergy offspring. She referred constantly to her status as a PK, a pastor's kid. One day, I met with her and her cadres. Each of them seemed to live or think about life on the edge of propriety. Some took to drink, others to drugs, a few to exaggerated sexuality. These forays into the taboo were an answer to their frustration proving again, "spare the rod" is not the answer to or for the disciplined "moral, Christian, Jewish" life. We were all aware of the extreme cases, the PK who served "time." The PK who became an inveterate rabble-rouser urging people to change their ways, to give themselves completely to God and yet, in the quietness of their own chambers, acted out the very things they denounced. Case after case came to my attention and more often than not, the one who was introduced to God because of fear of Him was the least of His stalwarts. One can't be dragged to love; one can only be gently embraced by its devotion and compassion.

Oftentimes it seemed my children were surrogates for me, the Rabbi, for the Jewish "Church," or any other negative feelings one finds in any urban setting directed by one group towards another.

They felt at times that people expected more of them because of their family status and situation. It was similar to the experiences of my earlier life. I recall an incident in 1939-40. I was riding on a bus and I wasn't wearing a head covering (hat or *kippah*). A man approached me and said, "How does a nephew of Rabbi Mendelson, the son of Rabbi Sky, dare to venture outside without a head covering?" My response was that I saw no need for it. "But," said he, "what of your parent and uncle's reputation?" I said, "They live their lives, I live mine. You want to wear a head covering, do so. I don't. There is nothing more to say." For a while, I was ostracized by a young orthodox youth group in Newark, (my home town). I questioned the authorship of Isaiah. I said there is Isaiah I and II. It was sacrilegious. My children didn't deny any of the faith's principles (at least not to me), yet, they had to bear the slings and arrows of being the children of a Rabbi.

Each one found his/her way out of the PK dilemma. Rina, my oldest child, spent some time in Israel, and speaks Hebrew fluently. She attended Ohio Wesleyan University. Upon graduation, she enrolled in the Jewish Theological Seminary education program. She lived in New York, in Florida, in Youngstown, Ohio. She met her husband, Bob, in Youngstown. They married and sired two children, Jacob and Thalia. Jacob has his music degree from Vanderbilt University, and Thalia is studying at Carnegie Mellon in Pittsburgh, Pa.

Uri, my middle son, graduated from Deering High, went on to Boston University and then to New York University. He is a banker by profession, currently employed by Siemens Finance. He, too, is married. His wife's name is Lori. They sired two children, Joshua and Lindsey. Both are struggling through adolescence. Ari attended Waynflete, went on to Brandeis, and George Washington University. He is married to Eve and works for Louden County, Virginia. They have a son and a daughter, Aaron and Amanda.

There are many stories to be told in their lives. Bob's conversion to Judaism, Rina's devotion to Jewish education, Uri's experience in banking, Ari's experience on the Hill and as a town manager.

Their collective bio's are a piece of Americana. Rabbinic children who found their own niche in Jewish and American life. It differs from the old days and the old country. In the old days, the lives of children reflected the lives of their parents. Both Ruth and I felt our children must discover their own mark, their own image. Rabbinic college existence is just one more aspect of human living and survival. It doesn't have a priority of its own. Faith, peoplehood, the old earmarks of Jewish existence, have taken a wide berth. It has its own definition. Because of Rina's experience, I became aware of an American Jewish phenomenon. The individual "Jewish" journey which seems to outshine, perhaps outlive, the collective journey of the Jewish people has its own momentum. It can't stop, nor can we halt it. One can swim with the tide and hope and pray some form of Jewish identity will remain.

"From my earliest days, I was blessed with a ripe imagination. Whatever I studied became alive for me. The Rabbis of the Talmud were never names on a page but thinking, questioning, doubting, and believing human beings. To them (and to me), the creative force that kept the world alive never disappeared. With this thought and feeling in mind, I always felt I lived a polar existence. On one hand was the reality of daily existence, on the other, my approach to life revolved around the concept of mystery."

MINISTRY

In the early years of my Rabbinate I resisted participation in intermarriages. At first, I was opposed to it. I considered the open marriage as the possible death knell to Jewish existence. As the years went by, experience, perhaps expediency and other factors seemed to remove a veil from my eyes. As I grew in my belief that life is a journey and we are always in a state of becoming, intermarriage is part of it. You can't close your eyes to life and its occurrences. You can't wish them away, pray them away or drive them away. The notion of who is the mighty one, he who never changes his mind, he who stands as a guardian of the gates, no longer "holds water." The mighty are the discerning ones who agreed with the alchemists of old, "the waste contains the gold." The difference is, new nuances, they produce the seeds of tomorrow.

All of my native creativity came to the fore. I seemed to be a bridge between the Jewish and non-Jewish communities.

I spoke up for the State of Israel. I, together with others, (such as Jerry and Rachel Slivka) addressed the Holocaust and its lessons for human history. I was invited to teach at the University of Southern Maine system. The governors of Maine appointed me to state commissions: Human Services, Maine State Parole Board, etc.

To me, one of the most significant highlights was the Temple Beth El art show. In 1961, quite soon after my arrival, Harold Nelson, of blessed memory, approached me. He said, "Rabbi, why must our major fundraisers be the Purim games." In Jewish tradition, Purim was the moment in the year when all guards are lowered and all standards are set aside. For it celebrates that moment in Jewish History (whether it was an historical event or a wishful myth) when Jews were rescued from extinction (check the Book of Esther). Up to recent times, it was the "Mardi Gras" of the Jewish world. Games of chance were permitted, an invitation of "Ahashuerus' banquet" the beverages (most likely alcoholic) flowed without end. In time (even at the staid Temple Beth El), it became a raw moment. Harold Nelson, the fine, refined gentleman, sought other means to fund the temple and its many worthwhile programs. I proposed an art show. I invited Peggy Osher, Millie Nelson, and Nancy Davidson Silverman to a meeting and asked them if they would chair the event. They agreed to do so. We met, we planned for many months. Peggy Osher prevailed on her brother-in-law, Barney, and he loaned us the core of the exhibit - original works by Renoir, Sawyer and others.

Millie Nelson, a patron of young Maine artists, approached many of them and they agreed to loan works for display and to provide works for sale. Nancy Davidson Silverman hurried and scurried. She visited galleries in New York City, Boston, and elsewhere and acquired for sale rare prints and limited editions. During the first 24 hours of the exhibit, we had sparse attendance. On Monday morning of the art week, I called the newspaper and prevailed upon them to send a reporter to view the exhibit. They hesitated and said a blurb had appeared a few days prior to opening day. I said to the editor, "but you haven't captured the true flavor of the exhibit."

My persistence was rewarded. A cub reporter was assigned the task of reporting on the exhibit. Fortunately, she was an art maven. She stared in awe and asked me again and again, "Are these originals?" I assured her the Jack Levine, the Sawyer, the Matisse, the Renoir were originals. She asked if I was sure. I removed the paintings from the boards on which they hung. She examined them front and back, ran to the phone and urged her editor to stop the press, to send a photographer. The afternoon edition was delayed, and we were given a two-page display. That evening and for the next five days, the temple social hall was overflowing with viewers. Holverson, the curator of the Portland Museum of Art in 1962 hung the show. It launched him, and it launched us. Suddenly Temple Beth El and the Jewish community were viewed differently. It was no longer seen as the relic of Old Testament days, but a vibrant, living branch of modern culture. I'm convinced the art show which lasted for 11 seasons was the catalyst for the explosion of culture in Portland. It influenced the public library; it led to the reorganization of the Portland Museum of Art. It stimulated greater interest in art, in music, in theatre and many other cultural benefits.

From my earliest days, I was blessed with a ripe imagination. Whatever I studied became alive for me. The Rabbis of the Talmud were never names on a page but thinking, questioning, doubting, and believing human beings. To them (and to me), the creative force that kept the world alive never disappeared. With this thought and feeling in mind, I always felt I lived a polar existence. On one hand was the reality of daily existence, on the other, my approach to life revolved around the concept of mystery. Recently, it occurred to me "mystery" contains within itself that which is yet to surface and that which is truly *"B'rumot Haolam"* (everlasting); never ending, never going away until it is integrated into the conscious part of one self.

It occurred two years ago. I was sitting writing at my dining table. I fell into a deep sleep and saw standing beside me a tall, handsome being. It had in its hand a flickering light. A benign smile crossed its face. It exuded warmth, comfort. It seemed to want to embrace someone or something, yet its body form was translucent. One could view it and yet not see it. I was amazed by the sight. I've wondered about it and can't find an answer to my questions: "Who is it? What is it? What does its kind, benign manner want to convey?" This image comes and goes. I know it bears a message. I've been prone to such images throughout my life. I thought at times it's a concretization of the Divinity I believe in and am forever seeking.

I have said time and again that I am not a linear thinker. I seem to have an innate linkage to all I meet casually or directly. I am convinced in all of these encounters a deep message is being conveyed. Mainly, "don't despair." In our life journey we encounter many sights and beings, none are final.

All are peripheral, leading to another and another. I dreamt a dream. Its core was the image of the "great God" being surrounded by nymphs or other winged creatures, drawing succor from its body. Its face was chiseled, i.e. had distinct features, yet seemed vague as if I were seeing it through a misty glass. It seemed as if It was sheathed in a cocoon. Yet it passed. You could see its breath. Its chest, its abdomen heaved. It stared straight ahead as if its world didn't surround it but lie within it. I wondered why it was there. Why did it appear in my horizon? Was I connected to it, was it connected to me. Many moments passed and I sensed a change in the atmospheric pressure of the place. Its shift, its focus was realigning. Is it a robot, or is it a living, pulsating human being. I tried to speak to it, but no sounds came out of my mouth, no movement of my body. Yet I knew it was there for me and I for it. Many silent moments. Suddenly I heard an intake of breath. I looked, its brow was wrinkled, and its eyes appeared. Up to that moment I sensed human features but couldn't see them. Now the eyes, the mirror of the soul came alive. My gaze shifted. I no longer felt drawn to this massive, chiseled, well-proportioned male body. I looked into its eyes. I saw something else. Little sparks of various colors, jumping, dancing, prancing. Each bit of color had tonal values. They sang and in harmony, they seemed to compose a piece of live music. Over and over again I heard the words accompanying the melody, the tone, the song. "*Haneshama loch, haguf shelach.*" "The soul, the divine breath I possess is yours. It belongs to you. I'm only a lessee. My body has been gifted to me and, in turn, the melody was gifted to my soul. My body and my soul are yours." But, then, I heard another phrase - *chusah al amelach.* "Be a shelter for all you have created." It was a strange request. It wasn't a prayer, a request for a few, but for all you have brought about

My reverie was over. I was fully awake. I pondered this episode. What is being said? I knew it was a universal statement. At last I was saying and expressing very deep feelings. "God, you are not here just for the few. You are here for the puny, and you are here for the massive." For if truth be told, neither puny nor massive can stand on its own two feet. There are moments when they seek shelter and you are the provider.

That vision occurred in the 70's. The entire decade was a trying time for me. From 1961 until 1972 was my trial run at Beth El. As I had predicted, the first period from 1961 until 1966 was the honeymoon. 1966 to 1969 was filled with criticism and from 1969 until 1972 a change in congregational leadership had taken place. Rabbi Bekritsky resigned and was followed by Rabbi Dworkin. He was young, dapper in appearance. Upon his arrival, he called on me. I greeted him and accepted him in a cordial manner. We discussed congregational business and I asked him if he had a plan for his congregation. He said he wanted to duplicate the congregation from which he stemmed. His Rabbi was Rabbi Joseph Ehrenkrantz whom I knew from my hometown, Newark, New Jersey. Rabbi Joseph Ehrenkrantz's father was Mordecai Ehrenkrantz who had been a thorn in my father's back. They both belonged to the *Shochtim* (ritual slaughterers) union. Ehrenkrantz was its president and chief labor negotiator. My father lived by the teachings of the Talmud, including its sense of morality in human relations. He avoided trying neighbors and deeply believed in negotiation not confrontation as the life lesson. We have many family stories illustrating his way of life. Among the *shochtim* (ritual slaughterers) and others involved in Jewish political battles, he was known as the scholar, at times considered naive for upholding the ancient Rabbinic codes. I sensed speaking to Rabbi Dworkin, the Ehrenkrantz approach; "Act tough, believe in your toughness and you will wear down your adversaries"

I asked Rabbi Dworkin, "Do you have an image or a dream describing the congregation you hope will eventually emerge?" He said, "Yes. A duplicate of Stanford, Connecticut. Its model is for me the model." How many families belonged to it? He said there were 700. "Are you aiming for such numbers in Portland?" "Yes." "Where will you find them?" "Here in Beth El."

I gulped. Here we go again. The breaking of walls, of boundaries. Rabbi Ehrenkrantz Sr. had displaced my father. Earlier in this memoir, I described the moment my father stood on a platform urging the customers not to patronize the market. I was sure Ehrenkrantz Jr. approached Stanford Jewry as his father did in Newark and I said to myself, "His protégé is going to engage in the same tactics in Portland, Maine." He did. Rabbi Dworkin would attend the Sunday morning breakfast *minyan* (service) on with application for membership in *Shaarei Tefilah* - the local orthodox congregation. His predecessor, Rabbi Bekritsky, vowed during the early stages of Beth El's being built, the foundation hole would never be filled and the temple would never rise.

My father survived Ehrenkrantz Sr. so I said I would survive Ehrenkrantz Jr's disciple. It wasn't smooth sailing. A group of Beth El'ers rallied and began to sing Rabbi Dworkin's praise. Some had gathered and hoped to convince the temple leadership that I was a "has been." The vote occurred in November of 1971. I was reelected by a vote of 3-1.

I suffered my first heart involvement the weekend after the vote. I was hospitalized for three weeks. The precipitating event took place at the annual Israel Bonds dinner. It took place at the temple on Sunday evening. That afternoon I went over to see how the dinner arrangements were faring. I walked into the kitchen and saw a man with beard and *payot* (side curls worn by the ultra orthodox Jews.) I extended the Shalom greeting and asked him, "Who are you?" He told me his name and said he is the *mashgiach* (the kosher supervisor) for the affair.

I asked, "Who appointed you? I am this congregation's Rabbi, and I supervise the *koshrut* of the kitchen." He answered, "The Israel Bond office hired me"

I called the organization and asked, "By whose authority did you appoint this gentleman?" The man there said he was told I was no longer Beth El's Rabbi and the orthodox won't attend unless there is a *mashgiach* in the kitchen since Beth El's "*kashrut* standards" do not meet orthodox standards.

"Don't you think decency called for your speaking to me and, by the way, I was voted in last Wednesday. I am the Rabbi at Beth El."

I was overwrought. Two doctors examined me and urged that I be hospitalized. During my three-week stay in the hospital much occurred. Attempts at reconciliation were made and one year later, I received life tenure.

I sensed at that point, some of my ideas were bearing fruit. Within the Jewish community, the idea of *Kehillah* (overarching community) was being floated. Unfortunately, we never had one or two philanthropists interested in Jewish survival as in other communities. Everyone seemed to be turf conscious thus preventing communal approaches to the problems of Jewish people living in Maine. Earlier (1950-1979's), the Jewish center movement, the Camp Lown initiative attempted to use the overarching approach.

From 1967 - 1973, Israel's survival served as a unifier in the Jewish community especially at Temple Beth El. Our youth group sponsored annual 7- 8 week pilgrimages to Israel. Many of our board members were involved in promoting Israel's viability to the surrounding communities. From its inception, many in the non-Jewish communities questioned Israel's right to exist. From the 1940's-1970's, the lack of response of America, and the rest of the Western world to the Holocaust put a damper on the accusers and questioners. Political correctness called for at least a sympathetic sigh when speaking of the Holocaust. But by the mid seventies, one heard skeptical voices, questioning the historicity of Holocaust movies and literature. I felt at times that I was defending the Jewish understanding of this horrendous movement in human history. I saw many possibilities and I responded.

At first the questioners were Jews. Where was God when this occurred? Or why did the world sit by silently without protest? More specifically, why did America close its doors? What prompted America's refusing the docking of the SS Hamburg. Why were they sent back feeding Hitler with additional propaganda? "No one wants the Jews. Not even Rosenfeld (Roosevelt). Some Jews asked why did organizations such as the *Agudath Yisrael* and ultra orthodox Jewish organizations block the admission of non-*dati* and non-*charedim* into Palestine? Why did they say Jews whose observance scheme differed from theirs weren't worth saving?

Questions were posed by many Jews and non-Jews alike. In some Christian circles, one sensed an attempt at *"Teshuva"* - repentance, return to civility. Some non-Jews, in order to show their disgust and dismay, provoked by the Nazi records, opened their doors to inter groups and interfaith activities. I received many invitations to speak in churches, in universities, in schools, both private and public. Some people, Jews and non-Jews, gathered and launched a study program, hoping to understand what triggered the genocide. What darkness lives in the human soul leading to mayhem, destruction and the death of so many innocent victims! Many asked, "Is this inevitable?" There were studies proving potentially many of us are persecutors, authoritative types, intolerant of all deviant behavior. Some insisted on "natural law" implying there is one inherent law that is God's law. Anyone who differs with this law is of the no-God world and stands under a cloud of judgment, destined to be annihilated.

This rationale has been accepted by some circles. Whole societies have been built on these assumptions. It led me to believe in the Western world, two poles were prevalent; one, based on the biblical notion of humankind descended from one archetype; the other based on the evolution of the species. The latter took into consideration various factors that precipitate change and "growth." The danger lies in the second approach. For it speaks of the survival of the fittest, thus encouraging the notion of "might makes right." While the former stresses "not by might, not by power but by my spirit," saith the Lord. Of course a working premise for me has always been the notion of "becoming." Whatever exists in this world is a result of unfolding. Nothing is by nature static. Various factors are forever interacting with each other precipitating constant change. Thus we begin with the archetype. Within it lies all that will eventually emerge and unfold, thus allowing for evolution.

It seemed to me by the end of the 70's the time had come for looking at all of life, all of nature in holistic terms. I sensed too much parsing has taken place. I was examined one day by a well-known urologist for prostate problems. (I was in my 40's.) While I was lying on the examination table, I felt great discomfort in my chest, lungs and heart. I told the physician about it. His reply was, "That's not my area of expertise."

While specialization might contribute to our greater understanding of the human system, it has abandoned the aspect of soul, which is the essence of the human.

In the 80's I became involved with holistic medicine. Dr. David Getson invited me to join the lay board of his new practice, and I agreed. My wife, Ruth, was deteriorating physically. Her cancer, her arthritis was taking its toll. In our early years, our family physician was Dr. Albert Aronson. We trusted him completely. He seemed to be at ease with the entire person. One could walk into his office and he immediately would sense, almost intuitively, the status of your body and your mental health. When he left his private practice and became involved with Maine Medical Center, my wife and I both felt a terrible loss. We went from physician to physician, never feeling at ease. After a while she was left without a general practitioner. So was I. But the angst, at least for me, prevailed. After a while, I attributed most things to my psyche, to soul angst. I attended the board meetings of our holistic practices and I availed myself of Dr. Getson's ministrations. He had as part of his practice a Polaris massage therapist, a dietician, a dentist, an acupuncturist, and a psychic. Each approached the human from their angle's viewpoint. Dr. Getson met with all of them regularly and in concert. The whole patient was addressed. Thanks to the massage therapist, I felt myself opening up and much of my pain was subsiding. Through the psychic, I delved into numerology and found its sister in *gematria* (mystical numerology), the ancient Hebrew version of the science and ideology of numbers. For three years, I read peoples' charts and proved to be quite accurate with my readings.

Ruth retired from Unum in 1987. We visited Paris. (I wheeled her in her wheel chair.) We went to Disneyland (same mobility) and we took the Trans Canadian Railway across the continent. In these few years, our care for each other grew. In the summer of 1990, we went to Tanglewood for the last time. She expired in December (Chanukah) 1990.

During the period of my involvement with holistic medicine, I became interested in the teachings of Dr. Carl Gustav Jung. I went twice to Zürich/Kussnacht for seminars. In the second visit (summer of '89), I met Dr. Hermann Ströbel and he became one of my late life mentors.

I retired from Beth El in June of '89. Linda Abromson chaired the event. Dr. Shorsch, Chancellor of Jewish Theological Seminary, spoke. Ari surprised me with the metaphor of my carrying him on my toes. Other highlights: Roz Bernstein crediting me with opening the doors for women - in the Rabbinate and cantorate. Of special interest was Prof. Bill Geogehagen's homily comparing me to Elijah, the spirit that came from nowhere and instills the God Presence into the moment.

Father Steve Foote participated as did Msgr. Charles Murphy. There were video messages from politicians (governor, congressmen, councilors, senators). It was a lovely evening.

Rabbi Seth Frisch succeeded me. It wasn't a friendly relationship. He was unpredictable. He left after four years, and I served as interim for two and one half years until Rabbi Carolyn Braun arrived. In the meantime, I remarried one and one half years after Ruth's demise to Helene Gerstein. It was a stormy few years. During this time, I helped found Seniors College which became known as OLLI (Osher Lifelong Learning Institute).

"Look for the self that's really you.
That is God within you. Once
you're in tune with it, you can follow
your path and respond not to the
world around you, but to the world
within you."

SENIORS' COLLEGE

Senior College was an outgrowth of where I was going. Dr. Pattenaude, President of the University of Southern Maine, had spoken to my late second wife, Helene, and had said that he would like to meet me. He wanted me to be on a University of Southern Maine community board.

I spoke to him and said, "There are many retired people like myself. Our heads are still working. Our curiosity is as strong as it ever was. And we'd like to have a place where we can come and study, peers with peers, without credits, without degrees, without papers."

"I'll think about it," he said.

I was after him for three years until one day he told me that he had spoken to his mother about my idea and that she thought it sounded good. That's how it began.

The first course that I offered in Senior College was "Spirituality as seen throughout the world."

In the early days there was not much of a definition to it. Although President Pattenaude was very supportive, he did not know what to do with us! We didn't fit in. We were not undergraduates and we did not follow a curriculum. Over time we worked out a *modus vivendi*. No one told us what we could and what we could not teach and our offerings covered a wide range of topics. Nobody censored us.

From the beginning we were governed by a council. At first it consisted of University personnel, who did not really understand what the Senior College was trying to accomplish and it felt like they were trying to control us.

We formed a board and I was asked to be Chair and realized right away that we would need some money to get things going. So I called up Selma Black, who had always been a trusted advisor and a close friend to me and to my wife. I said, "Selma, what should we do?"

She said, "Very simple. You find twenty or thirty people who will give you $100 apiece, and you'll have enough to get going. I'll give you the first $100." Within 30 days we earned 22,000.

We did our research. We went to Harvard and studied their model, and then we visited North Carolina and looked at what they were doing. We came to the conclusion that the best model for us was peer teaching. Instead of paid faculty we wanted volunteers, peers teaching peers.

The way Barney Osher came on board is a story in itself. His brother had died, and I officiated at the funeral. After the funeral he asked me, what I was doing these days. I talked to him about the Seniors' College. He invited his brother Harold discussed it with him and approved the program.

Negotiations began. Harold Osher gave us two and a quarter million dollars. The following year he watched us very carefully. There were constant visitors coming from California to see what we were doing. He was convinced that our model was the best model. We now have 119 OLLI (Osher Lifelong Learning Institute) sites throughout the country, and nineteen Senior Colleges in Maine alone.

The Senior College was the stimulus for this movement, and the University of Southern Maine gained much prestige because of their involvement.

My father was a man who never stopped learning. Even in his old age when he was very sick, not one day would go by that he did not read. He could hardly breathe, but when he went to his bookcase and took out a book and started to read, all of the sudden his disease was gone.

At this stage in my life I am having the same experience. There are times when I get blue. I have no family left. In case I get sick, who's going to take care of me? I worry about all those medical conditions older people are expected to develop. But then I start writing, I start reading, I turn the computer on. There is something wonderful and healing about learning. The Talmud says somewhere: "If someone feels that something in his head is not right, then he should get involved in learning."

I always seem to have a writing project. And when I have a thought I run to my desk and put it down. Otherwise I probably would feel some pain here and some pain there and worry where it's coming from. The next thing, I would be imagining the worst, and, who knows, might end up in the hospital, the victim of a self-fulfilling prophecy.

Look for the self that's really you. That is God within you. Once you're in tune with it, you can follow your path and respond not to the world around you, but to the world within you. That is the key.

The cross-fertilization that takes place in lifelong learning is wonderful! I think older people should continue doing what they are doing, and realize that the more you keep the mind going and the spirit going and the sense of soul going, the better chance you have for a long life. If you stop looking for pills to calm you down, and you start looking for thoughts to calm you down, you might go further.

I will end with a true story. A woman came over to me one day in Senior College and said, "I went to see my doctor yesterday. He looked at me, and he says, 'Oh, Mary. You look good. What have you been doing lately?'"

'Oh well, I decided I didn't want to be a couch potato anymore.'

'Fine. So what are you doing about it?'

'Well, I go to Seniors' College.'"

And he wants to know what Seniors' College is, so she explains it to him.

"Oh very nice, Mary," the doctor said. "Keep it up. It's doing you a lot of good!"

As Mary is leaving, she sticks her hand into her pocketbook, takes out an envelope full of all of her pills, gives it to the doctor, and says, "I don't need this anymore." And off she goes.

"My years in Maine were built on a premise: Each human, no matter of his or her origin should be entitled to a level playing field. Our Rabbinical tradition emphasizes this idea. At conception, one was created as an androgynous being. Definitions came later."

OUTLOOK

It happened many years ago. I was sitting on a subway train en route from my teaching assignments. I sat next to a redhead like myself. My fellow passenger began the conversation. He bemoaned the fact that this country with its abundant supplies is unable to feed the hungry. He faulted our capitalistic economy. If we could adopt the way of the USSR, its constitution assuring the essentials of life: shelter, food, clothing, and then all would share resources and life would be paradise itself. I cited the statistics of that day's *New York Times*. The article spoke of the great disparity between party officials and the masses in the USSR. He looked at me and asked me, "Do you believe everything you read? After all, you must realize that the press tends to distort the facts."

I shrugged my shoulders.

I said, "A plague on both of your houses!"

He then moved over, and craned his neck, trying to get a glimpse of the passage. Satisfied, he left in a huff and a flurry, making sure he expectorated on my shoes.

One sunny afternoon, Ruth and I went to Magnolia, Massachusetts. Rina was with us. Even at this age, she was attracted by colors and fabrics. We entered a children's store and browsed through infants' clothes. Whenever we took off the rack a pastel colored garment, Rina would respond. Her vocabulary was limited, but her wants were obvious. Little did we realize Rina's native dramatic sense. As she advanced in age and experience, this sense manifested itself in many ways. Rina's companions consisted of "live" friends, imaginary friends, and sympathetic friends.

One day, during the first year of her life, Rina was sitting in her stroller. Every so often she would point to something and call out its "name." Sometimes it was a "passing" recognition. Sometimes she would engage the object. It became obvious to Ruth and myself that Rina's imaginary world lived side by side with the conscious world. For Rina understood everything, the earth and the universe is God's residence. God is forever manifesting Himself. Her imaginary world, the world of fantasy, is God's world.

The early years of my rabbinate were filled with questions and puzzles. I never seemed to "get it right." Gloucester, Massachusetts, my first position, was of short duration and it was not filled with many successful moments. Newburgh was for me the *nadir*, the absolute bottom of my congregational existence. Alexandria, Virginia had great potential, but my naiveté got in the way. I didn't sense its vibrancy and possibilities. Bellaire, Texas yearned for a new definition of Jewishness. I was too caught up with my own growth or lack of growth to respond. Indianapolis, if Bill Greenfeld, my senior rabbi, had lived, I think I would have flowered there. But destiny directed me to the frontier world of Maine. From the moment of my arrival in 1961, to the present writing moment, my time here has been filled with moments wrapped in opportunity. In these 47 years, I have become acquainted with my inner self and have befriended my dragons. From these experiences, I have decided that the darkness of the moment becomes the sunlight of the future.

I've felt these many years that my family and I are living in God's sacred garden, surrounded by angelic personalities and witnessing daily acts of unsurpassed kindness. The Talmudic sages, in describing the efficacy of the Holy Land, said, "*avira d'yisrael mahkim.*" The very air of the land enlightens all who experience it. I have sensed this about Maine.

From my first day of arrival in August '61 until today I am energized by the kindly works undertaken for those who find life burdensome. Whether the hardship is financial, physical, or emotional, or spiritual, there are always some means available for amelioration of difficult circumstances. Behind these activities stands the good will of many, churches, synagogues, mosques and people of good will.

"Like a bull in a china shop," I went sailing into everything. Thank goodness I was able to contribute to the furtherance of good deeds, both for my enjoyment of helping others and for the benefit of those that were helped.

In the course of this work, I had been dubbed a liberal by many and a conservative by others. This was a comment on my life and my values. I am both, I say. Wherever humans live, humans give forever, seeking assurances that food, shelter, and clothing are available to all.

There were times when a "needy" one would approach me. The source of his/her neediness was his *mazal* (constellation of the stars) his/her good fortune. The sages taught, everything is subject to the intricacies of good fortune. Fortune itself is *mazal*, a combination or constellation of the stars. The *mazal* tell us what we can expect. And, if read correctly, it points the *way*.

During the course of my years in Maine I have sought and found psychics, astrologers and others who could read the present, past, and future and see or predict the ultimate outcome in order to decide what my own *mazal* will be.

I accepted quite early in life the rabbinic dictum, everything is in God's hands, except the way we see or regard God. To me God is essentially the mystery of life. Each of us has questions, each of us has doubts. Our questions and doubts are the story of our lives, as our beliefs and faith are the poems of life. As Carl Jung once said, "It is the shadow that helps the light emerge."

God, we sense, is the light we seek. In the ancient texts we read that God at creation time set aside "sacred light" to be awarded to the "*Zadikim*" (righteous) those who receive the Word. Each of us in his/her own way seeks the light of His Words.

The light of the righteous is wisdom at its peak level, the point of existence where all is in balance, when the contradictions of life have been resolved. This is when we can accept the light and the darkness of our lives and be one with it, when we can accept our strengths and not use them to conquer others. When, in the words of the depth psychologists, the shadow and the light, the hidden and the open each walk side by side, each contributes to the art of daily living.

Each day during my Temple Beth El tenure presented an issue in Jewish life, whether it was related to the Jewish education of our children or other life cycle events. One day a young mother and father came to see me. Newlywed, they were debating about the Jewishness of their home. They possessed all the accoutrements: a *mezuzah* (a container in which lies a piece of parchment with the passage of "Hear O Israel" inscribed) on the door, candlesticks used every Friday night on display. Their walls had select pieces of adornment. Their library contained many of the Jewish learning volumes. Yet they felt something was missing in the Jewish part of their lives.

I asked them to elaborate. "How do you define the 'Jewish part' of your lives? Is it a special section or compartment? Do you see yourselves as the carriers of many compartments? Do they interrelate, are they in harmony, or is your inner life a civil war, neighbors against neighbors, friends against friends, relatives on both sides of all questions? Is your Jewishness caught in such a maze, a part in conflict with other parts?"

The husband sat there with creased brows. The wife seemed to be thinking "yes" to all of my questions. She always felt that way.

I asked, "Were you the single Jewish kid in the classroom? The one who didn't follow the Christian creed? Whose parents told him or her one should never say praises to or about Jesus. During the preparation for the holiday program or whenever a carol was sung, did you mention Jesus' name? Do you still feel that way? Will you instruct your children not to utter Jesus' name?"

The husband interrupted me at this point. "That's not my problem" he said firmly. "Jesus is just another name. Everyone sees God in his own way, no matter what you were taught. God has never been a static word for me. When I say, 'oh my God', it is a response to a current moment. Another time it may refer to something else." I told him that is very

Jewish. In Judaism, God's ultimate name is YHWH, pro-
nounced "Adonay." It is related to the verb to be, to exist,
the extension the YHWH points to God. God isn't static,
God is always in a state of revelation, is becoming, and so are
we. The human creation is in God's image or form. We too
are in a state of becoming.

This incident took place in the 1980's before the populari-
zation of DNA.

In the early days of my Temple Beth El tenure I arrived by
sheer intuition at many concepts. Some were reflected by
rabbinic colleagues, and others were too radical. The concept
of the "evolving God" was one of them. The weight and shadow that is history and tradition often prevented me from
saying and doing what *I* considered to be Jewish. If you follow a strict traditional approach, then you are limited in your
expression. The traditionalist depends on the common notion
that one cannot digress from the teaching of the Forefathers.
The Forefathers are afforded higher status than all others.
The question of differing with the Forefathers was considered in some traditional circles as heresy.

Recently I defended the "fluid" approach. Mordecai Kaplan taught me that idea and I was intrigued by it. It became a
mantra for me. God is in a state of becoming and we humans
are too. Our bodies are forever changing. Our chemistry, our
biological parts, forever head in the direction of change.
Within recent years, our Rabbinical Assembly skirted the
identification of fluidity. A woman's role was strictly proscribed. When Mordecai Kaplan affirmed his daughter's coming of age as a *Bat* Mitzvah which placed her Jewish status in
life on the same level as 13-year-old Jewish boys, eyebrows
were raised. Mordecai Kaplan was by nature a pioneer. He
never denied "the ways of our Forefather." In fact, he felt the
code of Jewish Law had a value in our lives, in our Jewish
horizon. But it did not have a strict hold on us, it evolves. We
evolve, and our knowledge of God evolves, our way of life

evolves. God's evolution calls for a new consideration of the premises of our lives.

A few delegates at our Rabbinical Assembly addressed the question of ordination of female rabbis. The "way of our Forefathers" stalwarts opposed the idea. When it was adopted by our assembly and by the Jewish Theological Seminary, our mother institution, some of our colleagues left the movement (Conservative Judaism) and went over to those who would more closely follow the path of orthodoxy. Again, decades later when our assembly addressed the question of the ordination of gays or lesbians, some members of the Law Committee resigned. The seminary in Israel did not accept this ruling. A major spokesman for these changes was Rabbi Gordon Tucker. He said a review of 4000 years of legislation is necessary. There are new thoughts and new scientific findings all calling for reconsideration of what we believe is the way things should be done.

Being a "believer" in the notion that God and all of nature is in a state of becoming, I am not surprised at our committee's ruling. It is true that some of those on the committee differed and tried to place restrictions on gay and lesbian behavior. Yet Rabbi Gordon Tucker's reasoning was formally considered.

I believe God the Creator said at creation, "Now, human being, you contain something of Me within you. It's incumbent upon you now to go with the world and act as if you were its caretaker and its compass."

Many times in my life I have been both scolded and lauded: sometimes scolded for straying beyond the "law's" boundaries and other times lauded for being ahead of the times. In either case, I spoke up no matter the consequences. I refused to remain silent or remain on the side of the traditions if I did not agree with them. Sometimes I planted a seed and tasted the product of my success. There were other times that "I had to eat crow." Whatever was the way I acted, I thank God.

The Torah teaches us, be vigilant, forever ready and prepared to help another. Our sages understood this statement to mean helping another is not circumscribed. According to the Torah, the fellow resident who lives in your neighborhood is a member of your family, clan, or tribe, regardless of color or creed, regardless of the faith system he/she supports, regardless of the more destructive life choices he/she has made. You are related by DNA and other factors. You are, metaphorically speaking, all descendants of the first humans that resided on this earth.

In the recent immigration debate, some detractors forgot their faith. They said if we allow illegal Mexicans or other immigrants into the country, then the majority of the population will not be white, Christian, Anglo-Saxon. I say to them, so what? The founding fathers didn't ask that our nation be so homogenous, nor should we.

Believing in the worth of the human, I sought throughout my life opportunities not for the few but the many. The few, those with high IQ's, will make it in life. The many, those less endowed, still have a compensatory system within themselves that, when nurtured, will allow them to prosper as well. In the depths of my soul I knew it and understood it to be true when wisdom said "teach the young one according to his/her own potential". Unfortunately, our society on the whole is built on a closed program. We hear it in economic circles. Some are deserving of special considerations and privileges. They provide the machinery or the funds for the many. Don't reward the laborer or the inventor, only the ruling class. It completely negates the lessons of scriptures that say we are to love the least among us. Distribute your surplus wealth to the less fortunate. Whenever I spoke in such terms, I was labeled a socialist or a communist and not as someone who takes the scriptures' validity seriously. I still maintain that it is justice that man should pursue for the good of all, not just of the few.

Age has introduced a sense of sobriety in my mind. In my younger years I thought and felt that I knew "truth." Now,

I'm not so sure. I'm more than ever convinced that the maxim "God is in a state of becoming" is the working premise of my faith system. As He unfolds, so do we. As He defines himself and our universe, so do we identify ourselves. One can't escape from that "fact." I view all of life that way. One day, a former officer of Temple Beth El approached me with a question about Jewish law. He was seeking a clear-cut answer, a yes or no. Being a student of the Talmud, I knew one doesn't answer questions directly. There are in all cases variables that must be considered before a decision is arrived at. I tried to reason with him. He said uneasily, "Why can't you give me a direct answer, yes or no? Why must you hedge?" I told him that it is because life calls for such answers. According to Jewish law no one is ever found totally guilty of any transgression unless two witnesses can testify such and such is the case. All sides of the situation must be considered and only then may we try to find loopholes. For one never knows what determines any action.

I served for three terms on the Maine State Parole Board. The incarcerated appeared before our board seeking parole or early release from detention. I was frustrated at times when fellow board members seemed to imply that once sentenced you have "A Mark of Cain" on your forehead forever. Oftentimes parolees would break the rules of parole and become a recidivist.

One day I discussed this issue with the warden of the women's facility in Maine. She said many of the women felt the prison was a safer home than the streets and would therefore return to prison. Recidivism often was a reflection of this fact rather than the repetition of a crime.

My years in Maine were built on a premise: Each human, no matter of his or her origin should be entitled to a level playing field. Our Rabbinical tradition emphasizes this idea. At conception, one was created as an androgynous being. Definitions came later. Then they evolve as does our understanding of life of maturity, our views on creation and on God. One cannot, in discussing life and its many ramifications, insist on "one way" approaches, one set of humans deserving of recognition, salvation, redemption, etc. It's a God given gift to whoever listens to others.

The battles I fought for this principle were many. Civil rights, women's rights, the handicapped, the elderly, family rights for gays and lesbians, rights extended to everyone, no matter what their race, religion, gender, or sexual orientation may be. What you become is often beyond your ken. Having in my psyche the ancient genetic memory of Jewish mystics— their belief in "*Bashert*" (intended or anticipated)—I knew and accepted the correctness of this theory. It was part of my life's mystery.

My introduction to the "mystery" side of existence began early in life. During the first few years of my life, my father regaled me with tales of our Jewish ancestors. These stories took place in far away lands. Jewish people who had vanished many years ago lived in far away places. They inhabited distant lands. These stories were in the recesses of my genetic memories in magical facts and feats. I accepted those tales as if they were true pieces of recorded history. I was on the imaginative side, always accepting and yearning for the elusive, the unanswered, the almost lost and forgotten parts of our people's history.

As time went by my studies took form. In the core of the legends was the Pentateuch, the five books of Moses, or as we Jews call it, the Torah. Every day, every week, we study it closely. The discussion of it is the central activity of the Sabbath table. It is the weekly synagogue activity. The Torah has its stories, but our tradition teaches, don't look for chronological presentation in the Torah. It is not there. Don't expect any but human idiom when you read it. At an early age, I was reading the Torah in Hebrew with scholarly commentaries.

My head flowed with Aramaic writings. The Talmud, which is the core of the "rabbinic" writings" became my life long companion. Every Sunday morning I meet with a study companion and we spend a few hours studying text. The text itself is replete with the stories of my childhood. The mysteries, the fantastic moments of the great, and the ordinary.

In the Talmud one finds two groups of texts, The *Halacha* (detailed code or regulation) and the mystical *Aggadeta*. The *Halacha* is normative Judaism. It defines what you can and cannot do as a Jew. The *Aggadeta* is the mystical side, the "soul message" of our Jewish tradition. Some scholars give greater credence to the former. Many scholars caught up in the theories of the "mysteries of life" study closely the *Aggadeta*, the soul messages of our Jewish tradition.

As the years went by the "soul message" became clearer to me. In 1961 I offered a series of lectures at the temple on the concept of the soul in Judaism. This caused many of the congregants to take up the cudgel. They were rationalists and didn't believe any object of life lay beyond the five senses. "Seeing is believing" was a working premise for many of them. Since you can't see or measure the "soul" it doesn't exist. Initially I went along with them. In my heart of hearts, I felt there was *another* realm of experience, not necessarily subject to the view of the rational world. I knew it and I felt it.

Most of my undertakings, of social concern and otherwise, were prompted by some inner thrust. I call it soul work. Somehow I felt this or that must be done. Many times, I felt distance between myself and the world of daily news and activities. What seemed to catch the fancy of most families such as success in the sports arena, acceptance by "fashion queens," knowing and being seen with the right people, didn't drive me. I had waking moments when I was in the company of the high risers, the nouveau riche, but then my soul learning would pull me back. "He who pursues glory, finds that glory evades him."

One day I took a walk accompanied by one of my companions He was a neighbor and was obviously traveling on the fast road to success. At first, our conversation was chitchat. But then, it turned to such topics as, have you read this book or that one. We walked for 30 minutes. We covered the world in our conversation. Though we were friends, I sensed a difference between us.

I have had many similar friendships throughout my life. I sought deeper friendships. I looked for friends to whom I could reveal myself.

I've described in various places the ways and measures to overcome our loneliness. Some were socially acceptable, others were not. But I am convinced I came into this life with the message that I am not part of that crowd.

I've always wondered about the thoughts that pass through my head. I've pondered on the question of where do they start? Especially the imaginary thoughts.

Not too long ago I was sitting at my kitchen table, wondering about life. I asked myself, what's next? With no effort on my part, a scene emerged. I was standing at the bottom of an incline. To my right was a retaining wall. The incline led up to a path parallel to the wall. I climbed the incline. When I reached the parallel spot, a raven flew out of the sky and alighted at my feet. The raven spoke to me in human tones, with a human voice. It asked me what my destination was. I told it wherever life will lead me: I'm on a journey. The raven invited me to mount his back. I did. It flapped its wings and ascended into the clouds above. It flew and flew, through white, grey, and dark clouds. Suddenly a clearance opened in the sky, revealing a beautiful marble castle. The raven flew into the castle courtyard. When it touched ground, it turned into a human. I couldn't tell its gender, it wore a body long coat. It invited me into the castle. We entered the throne room, the raven-human sat on the throne and welcomed me home. "This is your place of origin. Three centuries ago you forged a bond with some here. You accompanied them to earth. The mission was to see how the humans are behaving on earth. You were disappointed and never became a member of their community."

As I pondered its message, I rose from my settee, walked through dark corridors, and came to a wall. I leaned against it with my left shoulder and it moved backwards. After a few moments, I heard sirens wailing and waves murmuring. The waves said to the sirens, "wailing and wooing will not change your situation, but the acceptance of fate will. Some things are in the process of changing and some things are stationary."

The sirens stopped and sighed. I, too, smiled inside of myself, for that was my life conclusion. Everything is changeable and the realization of this is one of final acts in one's approach to life.

This is my final story. My life has become the acceptance of the challenges and the quietness of waiting through the turbulent moment. With this, I end my story with the realization that we must pass our knowledge of this on to someone else.

Printed in the United States
209974BV00001B/160-207/P